DATE DUE

The Sexually Disturbed

The Sexually Disturbed

Treating Psychosexual Disorders

Averil Marie Doyle

PRAEGER

Westport, Connecticut
London

Library of Congress Cataloging-in-Publication Data

Doyle, Averil Marie.
    The sexually disturbed : treating psychosexual disorders / Averil
Marie Doyle.
        p.   cm.
    Includes bibliographical references and index.
    ISBN 0-275-94294-5 (alk. paper)
    1. Psychosexual disorders—Treatment.   2. Psychosexual disorders—
Case studies.   I. Title.
    [DNLM: 1. Psychosexual Disorders—therapy.   WM 611 D754s]
RC556.D64   1992
616.85′830651—dc20
DNLM/DLC
for Library of Congress   91-45565

British Library Cataloguing in Publication Data is available.

Library of Congress Catalog Card Number: 91-45565
ISBN: 0-275-94294-5

First published in 1992

Praeger Publishers, 88 Post Road West, Westport, CT 06881
An imprint of Greenwood Publishing Group, Inc.

Printed in the United States of America

The paper used in this book complies with the
Permanent Paper Standard issued by the National
Information Standards Organization (Z39.48-1984).

10 9 8 7 6 5 4 3 2 1

To my friend Charles Francis Dorlac, without whom the preparation of this manuscript would have been more difficult and less fun.

Contents

Illustrations

Acknowledgments

Carolyn Harlan, whose cheerfulness, patience and wholesomeness have been a constant support; Daniel William Doyle, whose perceptions added freshness to my view of myself and my work; Sharon Marie Doyle, whose enthusiasm and creativity inspired me in difficult moments; Tamar Marie Doyle, whose support and sweetness have to be mentioned; and Michael Mulhearn, whose good humor and insightfulness aided me immeasurably.

To my readers, who gave precious time on short notice: Thomas J. Audley, Daniel William Doyle, Jeanne Fish, Margaret Goldthwaite, Edward Levy, and Michael Mulhearn.

Special thanks to William Weiler, whose knowledge of publishing guided me at just the right moment.

Special thanks to Charles Blaine Van Gilder, whose illustrations enrich this work. Mr. Van Gilder is the director of admission at the Kansas City Art Institute and past director of Other World Children's Media; "Miss McFidgin"; and the Museum of Natural Curiosity for National Public Radio, Seattle. He has taught numerous adults and children to draw. His own drawings, sculpture, and ceramics have been shown nationally.

1
Influences on the Underlying Assumptions of This Work

Over three decades ago, while completing my doctoral dissertation, "Effect of Graduate Training in Human Sexuality on the Counselor's Ability to Deal with Sexually Related Problems in the Counseling Setting," I felt like a pioneer in the sexual wilderness. My design was used as the first graduate-level course in human sexuality presented by the Counselor Education Division at University of Missouri–Kansas City. The focus was mainly on sexual dysfunction and sexual identity, with sections dealing with what we used to call "desensitization." These sections were necessary because most of us were untrained in talking about sex in general, let alone explicit sexual behaviors. I became aware of the true meaning of a sex negative society and the pluralistic messages we are besieged with regarding all things sexual; that is, sex is attractive and desirable at the same time it is nasty and naughty. It is not socially acceptable to speak openly of sexual anatomy or behavior. Sexual arousal and orgasm are often shrouded in silence and mystery, so much so that many become confused and are ashamed and fearful of their natural body functions. Strong sexual feelings thus become a cause for alarm and create anxiety. For some, culturally induced sexual anxiety combines with other events and results in psychosexual disturbance.

Today, I am struck by the fact that I still live in a sex-negative society. The students and professionals who come to me for training and education still have essentially the same need for desensitization and sexual knowledge. I am no longer focused on sexual dysfunction. I have shifted my interest to gender dysphoria and psychosexual disorder as it relates to family dynamics. What I have discovered is that the general population, including a large percentage of medical educators and trainers of mental health professionals, experience negative attitudes toward the sexually disturbed. As a result they are less able to communicate with, and heal, sexually disturbed clients.

I hope that this portion of my work will motivate my colleagues to understand and help to overcome the effects of sexual negativism in all of us.

Conceptually, my work has been grounded in the developmental theory of Erik Erikson, and my work in regression therapy has been inspired by his insights. Karen Horney's explication on defense systems and the various mechanisms people use to defend themselves against pain constantly illuminates my understanding and clinical application of psychological theory. Like all others in our field, I have and will continue to be influenced by Father Freud. He knew how to keep his mouth shut in therapy, thus making fewer mistakes and letting the client do the work. Phenomenological currents are drawn from the spiritual reflections in the writings of Martin Buber and the earthy nurturance in those of Carl Rogers.

Literally all of my work has been affected by family systems theory. Clarification of the effect of family forces on individual sexual development is a major theme. Principles from learning theory or behaviorism, based on the work of John Dollard and Neal E. Miller (1939, 1941, 1950), and Albert D. Bandura (1968, 1969), have been invaluable in giving me understanding of the process of learning, forgetting, and relearning that is so much a part of understanding the sexually disturbed person.

Jacob L. Moreno's psychodrama has been extremely helpful in the formation of my work in regression therapy; particularly in the construction of the playroom, a setting within which recalling, restructuring, and reframing of past sexual trauma and mislearning is best accomplished.

A final word of self-disclosure. My own personality and confrontational style is the organizing principle of my work.

This has been both a blessing and a curse. It has at times intimidated and distressed my mentors, colleagues, and clients. As a child, I believed this quality to be speaking the truth, as I saw and felt it. As an adult, I still believe this. The truth both frightens and fascinates. It is an effective force in education, therapy, and everyday life, but it makes most people uncomfortable. Many shy away from it; others see it as rude and uncultured. I am thankful for that quality and the way it has affected my work and life.

2
Introduction to the Sexually Disturbed

Psychosexual disorder is common, as are sexual crimes, deviant sexual behaviors, and sexual mislearning. Perhaps no other area of human disturbance is so colored by misunderstanding and negative stereotyping. While much of human sexuality has been explicated, psychosexual disturbance has not.

This need is addressed by presentations of the sexual disturbances in story form. Case studies of female sexual exhibitionism, transsexualism, sexual aversion, ego dystonic homosexuality, gender dysphoria, sibling incest, and homosexual pedophilia are featured. I write from the vantage point of a therapist named after myself, but the persona of the therapist, Dr. Doyle, is a combination of many students, training associates, and consultees who have sought help in overcoming their own sexual biases and attitudes in order to help others. The problems Dr. Doyle encounters, the feelings she experiences, and the mistakes she makes are all part of the process of therapy. Her success in treating the sexually disturbed is as much a function of her commitment to the process of healing as it is to her knowledge and expertise in the field of sexuality.

Therapist reactions to sexually disturbed clients and to the process of therapy unify the chapters into a cohesive whole. The reader is inside the mind of the therapist as treatment is being formulated, and also has the opportunity to witness psychological theory as it is applied in the course of therapy. The personal thoughts, feelings, and reactions of the therapist render this book accessible in a new way to the general public, to consumers of mental health service, and to that segment of the population who hold their own sexual secrets locked in the pockets of the mind. Many readers who have yet to seek therapy because of their fears and biases against talking about their sexuality will benefit from reading about the process and meeting the sexually disturbed individuals who personify various psychosexual disorders. All the case histories are of people who, while suffering from a psychosexual problem, are functioning well in society.

These accounts of pain and mislearning experienced by the sexually disturbed provoke the reexamination of attitudes toward individuals with psychosexual disturbances.

Take Annie, the female sexual exhibitionist discussed in Chapter 4, who as a child witnessed sexual exhibitionism on the part of her father. As a result, she repeated the pattern in later life. Her behavior is shocking; she exhibits her genitals to strangers. Most people find this bizarre and offensive, but as you go through therapy with Annie, you come to realize that this sexual misfortune occurred through no fault of her own. Her behavior is a compulsive outcome of early childhood mislearning, which she seeks to undo. The pain she experiences trying to free herself from the deviant sexual behavior is enormous. Her persistence in trying to overcome her problem is noteworthy and admirable.

William and Marie, brother and sister in Chapter 9 who sleep together well into their adulthood, have developed sexual sadism and sexual masochism as a result of the guilt that they feel, and are confused and unhappy. They seek therapy because, without help, they cannot release themselves from the incestuous behavior developed in childhood and continued into their adult lives. Their psychosexual disorder is an extreme form of a common condition, sibling incest, which exists to a lesser degree in an unknown percentage of the general population.

Frank, the ego dystonic homosexual discussed in Chapter 7, desperately attempts to resist his homosexual orientation. He marries a woman, becomes a father, and becomes a substance abuser to shield himself from his sexual feelings for men. He is tortured by fear of discovery and by anger that he cannot be himself. Many men and women in the general population are forced into marriages and lifestyles by homophobic messages they have internalized.

Julie, the subject of Chapter 8, is gender dysphoric. She cannot accept her femininity because her alcoholic father and rolebound mother presented her with unacceptable models for both sexes. She believed she had only two choices; to be a male abuser like her father, or an abused female like her mother. Her father sexually molested her. The anguish she felt was so intense that it drove her, in later life, to attempted homicide. Julie is an extreme case of the reaction many children have to dysfunctional parental sex role models.

Roy, the homosexual pedophiliac in Chapter 10, has perhaps the most despised of psychosexual disorders; he was himself a victim of homosexual assault as a child, and he has repeated what he had learned. Did he have a choice, or was he compelled by erotic impulses he could not resist to sexually molest prepubescent boys who were first his students and later his victims?

Loretta, the subject of Chapter 6, experienced sexual aversion. She had sexually abused her baby sisters, after she had been repeatedly raped by her father from the time she was a child until late into her adolescence. She seeks therapy as an adult because she is terrified of her own sexual arousal; she is afraid she will succumb to recurrent impulses to sexually molest her infant son.

Ben, the transsexual in Chapter 5, is bitter and defensive because he feels he is a woman trapped in a male body. He is being cheated out of the female enculturation he longs for, and forced into the role and lifestyle of a conservative businessman. His whole life is a charade. Sexual reassignment surgery cannot give him what he had missed by not being raised as a girl.

None of these individuals chose their psychosexual disorder. All experienced early childhood sexual trauma or mislearning that interrupted the course of their normal sexual development. All have experienced pain and anguish as a result of what had happened to them. They represent a segment of the population who desperately need understanding and treatment. The therapeutic community has not been successful in treating chronic psychosexual disorders.

Does the barrier to successful treatment lie in the inability of therapists to overcome the culturally induced negative stereotyping that makes the sexually disturbed seem less than human?

3

Patterns from the Past: How Formative Experiences Take on Psychosexual Manifestations in Later Life

The psychosexual disorders of sexually disturbed adults can be traced to childhood mislearning. Sexual trauma in childhood often disrupts the course of normal sexual development.

When Roy, as a child, was sexually molested by his parish priest, he had no prior sexual learning and no cognitive framework to aid him in sorting through his confused reaction. Roy never forgot the erotic feelings; even as a child he knew that what had happened to him was significant. It was a totally new experience. What discriminating abilities his childish mind possessed were inadequate to absorb and process the multitude of sensations, thoughts, and feelings with which he was flooded. Roy's normal sexual development was arrested and then distorted by that experience. His sexual orientation and all subsequent sexual thought, sensation, and imagery were compressed and channeled into this single event, which he reenacted over and over in his adult life as a homosexual pedophiliac. Roy became a perpetrator of sexual crimes against prepubescent boys. Intense sexual impulses motivated him to repeat this offense until he was apprehended.

Roy's thought processes were also disordered by the sexual trauma. He had known Father Patrick, the priest, as a good man who had consistently helped his family during hard times. Father Patrick was also closely associated with God. When Father Patrick sexually molested him, Roy assumed that the erotic act of sexual deviance was good and even sanctioned by God. The erotic sensations were so powerful that they formed an indelible pattern in his memory. Later, as an adult, whenever Roy felt sexual arousal, the past trauma affected his behaviors. He was compelled to repeat the sexual event from his childhood, with himself as the perpetrator.

It was a truly formative experience. Roy developed a psychosexual disorder because of the confused pattern of unintegrated thoughts and feelings accompanying his initial introduction to eroticism.

The search for eroticism as it was initially felt is a powerful motivator for sexually disturbed people. In cases like Roy, where the child experiences extreme confusion and trauma, he may attempt to forget what happened, but the sensations and emotions are still linked. Cognition can be suppressed, but physiological traces linger. In some cases the sexually disturbed person returns psychologically, over and over again, to the developmental point of original disturbance, hoping to erase it or right it. Thus, the return to the same act of sexual deviance is a desperate attempt on the part of the sexually disturbed person to correct the distortion and resume normal sexual development.

Roy, the child, experienced so much cognitive dissonance when he was sexually molested by a priest that he himself experienced no guilt when he went on as an adult to sexually molest prepubescent boys. Roy associated Father Patrick with the conceptualization of good and God. This association had adhered to the sexual arousal and release he felt when he was sexually stimulated by Father Patrick. The question in my mind was, did Roy sexually molest the young students just to feel the erotic sensations? Or was he driven to repeat the same act to clear up his confusion, organize his thoughts, and erase the original experience because it so drastically altered the normal course of his development?

Questions such as this arise during the course of treatment when the client recounts the recurrent nature of the sexual impulses that drive him to replicate the original act. I remember listening to Roy, the adult homosexual pedophiliac:

> I was more excited if the surroundings were the same, you know, on a bed, in the home of the boy, parents gone, myself

an accepted member of the family. Trusted as a good person, like Father Patrick was to us.

I remember wondering about the word "excited." Did he mean genital excitement alone? Or was there also a regressive excitement that took Roy back in time to the precipitating event, to search for an explanation for what had happened to him and attempt to undo it, or make it right?

This thought has occurred to me numerous times in connection with clients who are psychosexually disturbed. They remember an event or series of events that occurred in childhood, involving what they believe to be the original sexual trauma, which they experience over and over again, sometimes in dreams, or in fragmentary image memories. The fragments come together into a cohesive whole, held in place by the memory of the eroticism. Fragments of the formative sexual experience manifest themselves in adult sexual behaviors.

Annie, the adult sexual exhibitionist, repeated approximations of what she had seen her father do when she was a child. She had not, at the time of the original trauma, comprehended the meaning of her father's genital exposure and masturbation, but it had been sexually exciting to her, and she had known he wanted attention. As an adult, she exhibited her genitals to strangers, seeking their attention. Perhaps this was an attempt to complete the act for her father and divest herself of the deleterious effects of the experience on her sexual development.

Thus, patterns of original sexual trauma or past formative experience take on psychosexual manifestation in the adult. I'm always struck by the anguished questions raised by the sexually disturbed. "What happened to me?" "Why am I this way?" The mystery of what transpires in the growth and development of the sexually disturbed is both urgent and haunting.

The child victim of sexual abuse complies with the adult's erotic invitation. The invitation to be sexually deviant is remembered and heard later by the latent, unconscious adult within the child.

Part 1
Therapy in Process

4
Annie: Sexual Exhibitionism (DSM-III-R-302.40)

Annie experienced recurrent, intense sexual urges and fantasies involving exposing her genitals to people, both male and female, whom she did not know. Sometimes she acted on these impulses, creating serious consequences for herself and her family. At other times she simply fantasized about exposing herself, masturbating to the arousal generated by images she conjured up in her mind. Afterward, whether she had actually exposed her genitals or only fantasized doing so, she would feel extreme guilt and distress. Her remorse and fear caused her to withdraw from social and professional activities. Sometimes she would not communicate with family members, friends, and/or work associates for several days at a time. It was after one such episode of withdrawal that she came to see me.

When I first saw her sitting in my waiting room, I was struck by how seductive she looked. Although her makeup and clothing were not blatantly sexual, there was an unmistakable "look at me" quality about her. She was seated on the edge of her chair, legs crossed, wearing a split skirt that exposed her leg well up to the middle of her thigh. My own preference for longer skirts and a more sedate appearance may have contributed to the total impact she had on me. I had long since learned that my own biases and value system had to be bracketed in order to evaluate and treat my clients effectively.

"I'm Doctor Doyle," I said, extending my hand.

"Call me Annie," she said, rather flippantly.

After we entered my office and seated ourselves, her manner seemed to change. She glanced at the diplomas and certificates on my wall, at the oriental rug and the leather couches, and asked, "How much is this going to cost me?"

"My sessions are $90. Is that a concern?"

She laughed. "Not really. I don't give a damn what it costs if you can help me."

"What do you want help with?" I asked.

She sighed and fell silent. Tears came, but no words.

I waited.

She smiled, trying to cover her pain. I looked at her, knowing my eyes reflected her feelings.

That seemed to reassure her. She stopped struggling and started to sob. I nodded a slight affirmation and paced my breathing, so that it was slower than hers and barely audible. I was on her track, and she could feel it.

My sessions last for fifty minutes. Annie spent all of the first session crying. There were very few words. At the end of the time, I told her I was glad we had made contact, and suggested we reschedule and talk about her feelings. We set up an appointment for the following week. She wrote me a check, thanked me, and left.

I didn't speculate about what her problem was, but I wondered if she would return. She had experienced a temporary reduction of her anxiety and felt that I was supportive.

Annie did come back the following week, and every week for almost two years. She was ashamed of her sexual impulses and behavior, and most of all of her compulsion to expose her genitals to strangers. It took her several months to tell me the extent of the problem. She was testing me. Could I listen to what she had to say without condemning or judging her? And could I then help her with her uncontrollable impulses?

There was a problem for me, but not in being judgmental. My previous experience with treating sexual exhibitionism had involved mostly male clients, many of whom obtained their strongest arousal responses by startling or shocking female victims. With few exceptions, the exhibitionists had not sought further sexual contact with their victims. I had also worked with numerous homosexual pedophiliacs, who after exposing themselves to young boys, followed that behavior by actually sexually molesting their victims.

Female exhibitionists are more difficult to detect and treat, because our culture encourages females to expose themselves to attract and excite males. Many normal females are confused about how, when, and to what extent they have societal approval to expose their private parts. It is also difficult to view the average male as a victim, because the popular cultural stereotype depicts males as always ready to participate in sexual activity.

But Annie had victimized males, and females as well. She had startled and shocked them, and in some cases had followed up with sexual interaction. She had never exposed herself to a child, nor was she aroused by the thought of doing so.

Since Annie was guarded in the early stages of our work, she did not reveal the extent of her disorder. It was unclear whether we were dealing with extreme female role behavior, which is not really classifiable as pathology, except for the anguish and dysfunction it obviously caused her.

Annie described how she would position herself, seated, with her skirt arranged in such a way as to expose her genitals. She would wear neither underpants nor pantyhose, so a clear view of her genitals was possible. She did this in airports, bus stations, restaurants, schools, and business places — any place that would maximize the shock or startle reaction of the victim. Usually she attempted no further sexual activity with the stranger, but on several occasions, when she did not get the response she wanted, she approached the victim and solicited a sexual encounter with him or her.

At no time did she solicit money or seek ongoing contact with her victim. Her arousal response was generally dependent on the reaction of the stranger. Excitement and resolution, that is, orgasm, came when the victim fled or became sexually aroused. It seemed to please Annie to think she could scare and arouse her victims at the same time.

There were other ways that Annie would expose herself. Sometimes she would wear a bathing suit to a swimming pool, sit on the edge, and wait for someone to swim by. She would then pull the crotch of her suit aside, spread her legs and look for the awaited response.

On occasion she would enter a fitness center and go into the women's shower room and dressing area. She would engage a woman in conversation and slowly start to undress in a provocative manner. In these incidents, the victim would initially be uncertain about Annie's intent. When it was no longer possible to mistake Annie's deliberate exhibition of her genitals, the woman would usually try to ignore it, make some excuse, and flee. This would excite Annie.

The first stages of therapy involved building trust for Annie and gathering information for me. She benefitted from talking about her feelings and behaviors. It provided anxiety reduction. We always focused on the problem and did not deal with other aspects of her life to any appreciable extent.

I drew her into the treatment process by asking what she thought would help her the most. We could focus on extinguishing the behaviors and/or understanding the causes.

"I need to know what went wrong with me. Why am I this way? How crazy am I? Should I just give up and kill myself?" We decided that Annie's distress would be alleviated by looking back through her sexual history for experiences and reactions that had contributed to her condition.

Instead of having her fill out the usual sexual history form, I asked her to tell me what she could remember about the development of her sexuality. I was deliberately vague, so as not to limit or structure her responses. At the outset of this exploration, we also decided to attempt prevention of further acts of exhibitionism by having Annie substitute masturbation to fantasies of a more appropriate nature. She would imagine herself in an ongoing sexual relationship with a person she knew and cared about. She could imagine herself wearing provocative clothing and undressing and showing her body to entice involvement. This way we would be conditioning her toward a more normal arousal response, which we hoped could eventually be transferred to a real relationship.

Annie progressed slowly at first in remembering anything relative to her early sexual development. She thought her childhood had been "mainly" normal and "fairly happy." She was an only child, raised by parents who seemed to love her. She remembered sometimes sleeping with her parents until she was about nine or ten. She had enjoyed doing that and reported having had "warm, tingly" feelings in her genitals when she was in bed with them.

As we talked I got the feeling that she was editing her responses or withholding information that did not fit with the image she wanted to portray. When we talked about her father, she said he was "gone a lot," and sometimes drank "too much." I suspected child abuse. The combined effect of her seductiveness and the regressed, little-girl impression she made, brought that to my mind over and over again.

Dr. Doyle: Annie, how much touching was there in your family?

Annie: None. I never saw my parents kiss or hug.

Dr. Doyle: I'm wondering about your parents' attitude toward nudity?

She was silent. I said nothing. She looked down, sat very still, and remained silent. She didn't move at all, like a small animal immobilized with fear. I had seen rabbits like that, when they were frightened, too scared to move. I knew if I broke the silence the moment would be gone. The anxiety would be gone and I would have to start all over again to rebuild it. I said nothing and remained still. There was no movement in the room. Only ten minutes went by, but it felt a lot longer. I wanted to cough. My throat was tickling. I silently modified my breathing to relieve the tickling in my throat. It worked. I began to relax, but maintained my stillness and silence.

Then, slowly, tears began rolling down her face. She held her position and remained soundless. I was very tired. It was close to the end of the hour. I wanted to move, stretch, reclaim my own identity. At this point I was no longer within her internal frame of reference. I was centered on myself and could feel my own feelings, but I didn't give in to them. I continued to reflect what I saw in her, but it was difficult, and I was afraid I couldn't continue.

Then she moved, just slightly, to wipe her tears from her lips.

She looked at me. I saw such intense feeling in her eyes that I once again moved into her feelings and reactions. It was easier now, because I didn't have to attend to my own sensations and feelings — they were suspended again and I was on her track.

Dr. Doyle: Say what you are feeling. Your eyes are seeing something. What is it?

My personal awareness flooded back. I thought I'd said too much. I had asked for her feelings, told her I saw something significant in her eyes, and asked her a question. Too much; it would confuse her. My students would get a C– for this!

But she was responding to something else, to her own memory, or perhaps to my intensity and caring. Miraculously, she began to speak. She was looking down again. "When I was little, my Dad used to do this crazy thing. He would sit across the room from me, unzip his pants and pull out his penis. Then he would look at my mother, but she wasn't watching. She would be watching TV, reading, or sewing and would never look up. He would rub his penis until he came. Then . . ." Her voice faltered and she looked at me.

Dr. Doyle: Then . . . ? (repeating her last word).

Annie: I can't remember. I'm tired. Isn't our time up?

Dr. Doyle: Yes. Will it be hard for you to stop now? What you've done today is very important.

Annie: I know. I'm tired. See you next week.

I was glad she was ready to stop. I was tired too. We had made a breakthrough, in spite of my blundering responses. Twice during that session, I had made a double response. A question followed by a statement. No room for the client to answer. (Counseling 101.)

From this time on, Annie talked about her father's exhibitionism over and over again. She was trying to understand and integrate it. She had never spoken of it before to anyone. Although both of her parents were still alive, she had never mentioned it to them. She was still afraid, just as she had been when she was a little girl and first saw her father expose himself.

One day she came into my office looking very unlike herself; no makeup, gray sweats, her hair pulled back in a braid instead of loose around her face, as she had always worn it.

I said nothing about her altered appearance, just looked at her and waited.

Annie: I dreamed about it last night. I was looking at my Dad while he did it. He was looking at my mother. I woke up feeling excited. I think I had an orgasm.

   (She started to cry, face down, head in her hands.)

Dr. Doyle: Annie, did he know you saw him?

She had never addressed that point before. I had wondered about it many times, but had not asked. I didn't want to lead her or plant a suggestion — either way — about whether her father's exhibitionism was directed at her. But it was time for her to clarify his intention toward her. Was he using her, or was he focused on her mother and oblivious of Annie's presence?

Annie (still crying): He never looked at me, but he knew I was there. Maybe he didn't mean to hurt me . . . He never looked at me. Does that mean . . . ?

At this point, words failed her. She cried louder and louder. The sobs trailed off into wails. She drew her body up in a fetal-like position. I was in the presence of the child Annie, that little girl who years ago had sat so still on the sofa watching her father expose himself. Only this time, with me, she let herself feel the confusion and fear. And she let herself move, draw her body into a self-protective fetal position. She cried for the remainder of the session.

As I reflected on the session and its major choicepoint, I was glad I had not pursued the content issue of what her father's intent had been. I needed to know, of course, as she did, whether she saw him as victimizing her or whether she had just been there, in or out of his conscious awareness during the act of genital exposure. Had I pursued it, that clarification, although highly significant to treatment, would have postponed the integration of feeling that had occurred by simply letting Annie cry. Her crying was a delayed reaction to the confusion and fear that she had not been able to express when the incident really occurred. This made it possible for her to explore the issue later, at a cognitive level, and eventually mobilize enough courage to talk to her father.

By this time, after fourteen months of therapy, Annie was no longer experiencing the recurrent urge to expose her genitals to strangers. Her arousing fantasies or dreams involving exposure also diminished and finally stopped. There were, however, infrequent dreams of the incidents. Her father would, in the dreams, expose himself, masturbate, look at her mother and . . . he would look at Annie. . . . This part she was uncertain of. She would then awaken feeling fear, but no arousal.

Annie wanted to know what had really happened. She was afraid to ask her father. Would he deny the entire incident? Would he laugh at her? Would it help her to confront him? She tried to get me to decide for her.

Annie: What shall I do? Will it help me to talk to him?

Dr. Doyle: Annie, I don't know. You have to decide for yourself. What do you think?

Annie: He'll get mad. We never talk about stuff like this. What will my mother think?

She would fall silent, sit very still, and wait for me to answer.

I knew I could persuade her to do this by asking her what she would say if she decided to confront him, but instead, I asked her what she was thinking and feeling, directing her thoughts to herself. She resisted again and again. I felt her trying to manipulate me.

Annie: You used to help me more. I'm not getting much out of therapy now. I'm stuck.

Dr. Doyle: Annie, stop trying to get me to do your work.

She was furious! All of the rage she felt toward me and probably toward her mother, came out.

Annie (screaming): Why won't you help me? All you do is sit there. Help me!

She picked up a pillow from the couch and threw it at me. It hit me in the face and dislocated one of my contacts. The pillow landed on the floor beside my chair. Another choicepoint. Do I respond from out of my own frame of reference or join hers? Either might work; that is, either might keep her on her track and encourage the discharge of her pent up feelings. I chose to respond from myself, as a more nurturing, responsive mother than Annie had ever had, since she was regressed and deep into the transference. I got up from my chair, slowly moved toward her, and knelt on the floor beside her.

Dr. Doyle: I want to help you, Annie. It is not right for you to be in such pain.
Annie: If only she had moved, or said something or stopped him, but she just sat there watching television.

There was no need for further response from me. Annie continued, "That happened many times. I would be so scared. I wanted her to look at him so he would stop, but she never did. I don't even know if she knew."

Annie started to cry, and leaned toward me. I held her. She cried quietly for a long time. I was tired. I couldn't see the clock, and I never wore a watch. Finally, she pulled away. I was glad I didn't have to move first; I didn't want her to feel rejected.

I knew I had to refocus her on the issue of confronting her father. Amazingly, she did it for me: "I have to confront both of them, don't I?" I just nodded slightly in affirmation.

Annie did talk to her parents. She did not rehearse what she would say; she was confident that the right words would come. At first her father denied exposing himself or masturbating in front of her; then he changed his story after Annie told them about her own acts of exhibitionism. He then said he had thought she was asleep. He told Annie how sorry he was that he had given her his problem.

Annie's mother also denied having been aware of what her husband was doing. She acknowledged that she had known that he wanted sex and was looking at her, but she "never dreamed" he had his penis out. She said she would have stopped him for Annie's sake had she known.

I asked Annie if she believed them. She said it didn't matter, she felt better because they had talked. The reality of the incidents had been confirmed and integrated for her.

We met only a few times after her encounter with her parents. She didn't need much consolidation. The issue seemed resolved. She no longer had the impulse to expose her genitals or startle strangers. My work with her was finished.

Years later I received a Christmas card from her, saying she was in therapy with her husband to improve her orgasmic response. I felt good that she had progressed to the point where she could have a normal sexual relationship, with minimal difficulties.

I have known many Annies, who as children were sexually traumatized or abused in some manner. They never received treatment or spoke about the anguish they had experienced. The result was confused learning about sexuality. Convoluted thoughts and images in the childish mind developed into pathology. In most cases there had been an unintegrated sexual event that terrified the child. Not being able to explain or understand it, the child was left with an overgeneralized anxiety relative to sexual arousal. Psychosexual disturbance developed, and abnormal behaviors resulted. Practiced repeatedly, these behaviors became entrenched to the point where they would yield only to targeted, in-depth therapy.

5
Ben: Transsexualism (Homosexual 2 Same Anatomic Sex, DSM-III-R-302.50)

Ben's hatred of his anatomic sex was so great that he once placed his genitals in a drawer and slammed it shut, in hopes of injuring himself so much that his penis and gonads would have to be removed surgically. Although he had read a great deal about sex change operations, he seemed to believe that it could never happen to him. The cost was too high, and the surgery was elective, so insurance would not cover it.

After the self-mutilation attempt, Ben was forced to see a urologist, who referred him to me for counseling. I knew nothing about him other than he had traumatized his genitals.

Sitting in the waiting room, he was rapidly turning the pages of a magazine without looking at them. He was also sucking on a piece of hard candy from my dish on the table. Slim, bottle blond, dressed like a conservative businessman, he emanated anxiety.

Dr. Doyle (holding out my hand): I'm Dr. Doyle.

Ben: Ben. Thanks for seeing me.

We walked into my office. Closing the door, I sat in my chair and looked at him. He was embarrassed because I knew what he had done to himself. I think he felt naked.

Dr. Doyle (smiling a little): Just start to tell me about it, Ben. Anyway it comes out is okay.

During the course of our sessions I learned that he had ferreted out and read every article I had ever written, as well as my entire doctoral dissertation, including appendices. He was motivated by basic mistrust and a consuming desire to learn everything he could about himself and his condition.

Anxiety and depression had driven him to a suicide attempt earlier in the year. He felt as if he were a woman. His sexual arousal response was to males, although he had experienced ongoing sexual relationships with different women, with whom he identified. Usually, he imagined that his penis belonged to his partner and that it was he who was being penetrated.

At first I mainly listened and helped him sort through his feelings and clarify his thoughts. I made a lot of eye contact and did not hesitate to offer empathy and support. Eye contact was difficult for him at the beginning.

Dr. Doyle: Look at me, Ben. Look at me.

Ben (head down, flushing): I know, I know. It's just that you have all the power.

To myself, I thought, "Only in your mind, Ben," but I did not say it. I knew that he was enjoying his powerlessness, a relief from being male and having to be in charge.

Was there anything sexually arousing in that? Too early in our relationship to ask. I didn't want to make him more defensive.

I was later to learn that Ben often experienced the thrill of surrender during therapy. He wanted so much to be a woman and enjoy "being taken" that he imagined it happening whenever he gave up control, even verbally in our sessions. He loved to talk; highly intelligent and artistic, he used words to fill up our time. Repetitive and redundant, he measured out and released his anxiety in bits and pieces. When he felt safe enough, he would yield to my intervention and let me guide and direct him through the maze of sexual confusion. His thoughts and feelings about sex seemed to be linked in a haphazard manner. Accustomed since childhood to hiding his deep wish to be female, he did it with me in therapy. Whenever he gave up his defense, he experienced such relief that it approximated the thrill of orgasm. This bothered him.

Ben: I dreamed I had an orgasm in your office.

Dr. Doyle: Tell me about it.

Ben: It's obscene to even think about doing that in your presence.

Careful to keep it on a professional level, at the same time I gave Ben permission to speak openly about the sexual feeling.

Dr. Doyle: Most people have a genital response when they talk about sex.

Ben: Do you?

Dr. Doyle: Sometimes. I talk about sex so often the magic is gone.

To augment therapy I asked Ben to keep a journal, or write to me in between our weekly meetings. He did this. Every week, two days before our session, he would leave a thick envelope in my mailbox. I told him he would not get his writings back. I felt that rereading his feelings, once he had expressed them, might prolong his confusion and maintain his anxiety and depression.

After about four months of talking and writing, Ben's acute discomfort was gone. He had been restored to his precrisis level of coping. He had acquired more effective ways of expressing his feelings, as by using journals. He was functioning at a higher level in his job as an account executive in an advertising agency, a position for which he was unsuited and overqualified. His personal relationships with his family had improved.

His basic issues had not been resolved. I had referred him to our staff psychiatrist, who did not believe medication was indicated. Ben was certainly not as self-destructive as he had been when he attempted to mutilate his genitals. Intensive individual therapy was needed to treat the psychopathology associated with transsexualism. Ben would continue to encounter problems socially and occupationally, because he was forced to live as a man while every ounce of his being cried out to be a woman. We had reached a choicepoint in therapy. We met to decide.

Ben: I don't want to open up another can of worms. I'm just beginning to sleep at night.
Dr. Doyle: You deserve a rest.

I did not seek to persuade him. Ben's condition was chronic. He had felt like a woman encapsulated in the wrong body for over four years. Sometimes the course of this disorder remits spontaneously, but this is rare. I did not think it would happen in Ben's case.

Ben: I can't afford further therapy, especially since you don't have a sliding scale.

I was aware of the need to bracket. Clients often make sarcastic remarks about my fees, which I, of course, believe are reasonable. This time it evoked a feeling of martyrdom in me. I felt unappreciated. I remained silent. Looking at him, I pondered my next move. It came to me. Ben's can of worms included exploring his homosexual feelings. We both knew that homosexuals often present themselves as transsexual because they cannot bear the pain of being gay. Ben's convoluted defense system certainly left room for that. I knew it would cause Ben pain to explore that issue. The timing was off. I wasn't certain that it was not an attack in retaliation for the crack about my fees. I remained silent.

Ben: You don't think I'm ready, do you?
Dr. Doyle: Maybe you are and maybe you're not. These things are hard to call.

Ben decided to terminate therapy and utilize his new coping skills to resume his life as before. He felt strong. At the end of the session, he thanked me for my help and offered me his hand. Then he took a few steps forward. He hugged me; there were tears in his eyes. I was struck by his vulnerability and openness with me. There had been no previous touch between us. It seemed significant that he had reached out to me. I had done good work and I had a feeling he would be back.

Five months later, Ben called and came in for an appointment. He had asked for and received a promotion and transfer to a different division of his company. He was now in a position that utilized his abilities more fully and allowed him to express his creativity. He had received a substantial increase in salary and had decided to invest it in therapy.

I asked Ben to tell me how he explained his transsexuality to himself. I wanted to know what he believed had caused or contributed to his sexual identity disorder.

He started with blaming his parents, listing several factors: how shallow and unfeeling they were, how overprotective his mother had been, how his grandmother had been the only one who had really cared about him.

Too external; nothing about his feelings in response to those factors. He had to reach deeper inside himself if we were to make progress.

Dr. Doyle: Bitter and blaming. Are there deeper feelings?

My words interrupted his harangue. I wasn't going to let him rant the whole hour away. Too vague and circuitous. He was past getting any cathartic benefit from that. He had to face his fear.

Ben: What shall I talk about? (Pleading.) Get me started.
Dr. Doyle: Your sexual attraction to men, cross dressing. What you are feeling right now. Take your choice.
Ben (gratefully): Thanks for the direction I can't do it myself.

Was he manipulating me? Probably. But it didn't matter. I had to get him started. He settled down on the floor between my two couches, where he liked to sit. I sat on the floor also, taking his lead. His defensiveness subsided.

Ben told me of cross-dressing when he was a child; wearing his mother's clothes, feeling like a girl rather than a boy. He also remembered coming home once and finding his older brother clad in a dress, sitting on the living room sofa watching television. His brother retreated immediately to his room, and they never talked about the incident. Ben's brother was now married and had several children. He was eleven years older than Ben. They usually saw each other only on holidays and special occasions. Ben obviously took comfort from the fact that his brother was also confused about his sexuality.

Ben: It was the parents. They fucked us up to the max, with their warped genes and warped values.

The bitter, blaming tone had returned to his voice. This time I just listened. "The parents," as he called them, had been concerned about their "old money" position in the community. Neither one of the boys had been permitted to play outdoors. They had only good clothes. Nothing to play in or wear around the house. This meant they were always supposed to be on their good behavior, meeting the role expectations for young males of the elite. The expectations were sissyish. Mother wanted their shirts, pants, and socks to match, and Dad wanted their shoes polished at all times.

Ben's description of his childhood fit the profile for transsexualism, which usually develops within the context of a disturbed relationship with one or both parents. Knowing that Ben had read portions of the DSM-III and DSM-III-R pertaining to transsexuality made me suspicious. He was not above trying to erase all doubt in my mind that he was homosexual. I kept getting the feeling that he was homosexual and afraid to admit it.

Dr. Doyle: Ben, are you trying to con me?

He looked at me a long time. Then he nodded yes.

Ben: I'm sorry. I should have known it wouldn't work. It's just that if I can't convince you, I can't believe in myself.

Feelings of martyrdom arose within me. I did not bother to bracket them. I didn't deserve this; what a waste of time, I thought. I was disgusted. I compensated by breathing softly and remaining silent. Ben went on trying to explain himself. He had no idea of my internal state.

Ben: Now that I'm getting close to having the money to pay for re-assignment surgery, I'll need a referral from you. Will you help me? (He was disclosing his motivation for the con.)

Dr. Doyle: I'll forward your records, and do everything I can to assure that you get appropriate treatment, but Ben, stop trying to stack the deck. It can't help you. Let's just deal with the truth where we find it. (I was moralizing and I knew better.) Tell me about your sexual interest in men.

Ben: It's because I feel like a woman.

Dr. Doyle (with a slight nod of yes): You want men to be attracted to you, aroused by you.

Ben (smiling, pleased with my response): Yes. I want it coming at me, I want to know how it feels.

Dr. Doyle: How can you make that happen?

Ben: I can cross dress and go to a gay bar, but . . . (He fell silent.)

Ben had thought about doing just that many times, but he had an irrational fear of arrest, ridicule, or worse. Most of all, he was afraid of discovering that he was homosexual. Internalized negative feelings about homosexuality, combined with consistent messages from "the parents" about the need to maintain an appropriate image, immobilized him. Ben's fear and shame were overwhelming. I had my own doubts. Was it right to encourage him to join a counter-culture, the gay community? Thus far in his life he had related sexually only to women, though in his fantasies he had reversed their genders and freed himself from his penis.

It was right to help him find his truth. My responsibility was to reflect and clarify his feelings. The decision was his own.

Dr. Doyle: Your fear will diminish if you tell yourself that you will always have the freedom to choose. . . . You don't have to live a gay life. (Not a great response, but adequate.)

Ben: Actually, I've already dressed and driven by the gay bar on 7th Street. I think I'll wait until next week, it's Halloween.

Ben did cross-dress and go to a gay bar on Halloween. He was terrified. He stayed just long enough to have one drink. He progressed slowly. Redecorating his home, he eliminated all masculine or androgynous furnishings. From photographs he showed me, it was clearly feminine. Shades of pinks and rose, with touches of lace. Somewhat Victorian, reflecting the pretension of his family of origin.

Then Ben met a woman. Oddly enough, she was one of my former clients, a lesbian I had treated many years previously. Neither Ben nor I were aware of this coincidence for several months. "She's the sort of woman that drives a Porsche and slams it into second," he reported. "She drinks martinis."

He was very enthusiastic, as he had been in the past with other women with whom he could identify.

Dr. Doyle: Tell me how you feel when you are with her.

Ben: Happy, upbeat. We laugh a lot.

Dr. Doyle: Sounds as if the woman in you is freed and you can be yourself.

He looked at me with tremendous gratitude. I had seen that expression on his face before, whenever I had referred to the woman within him as if she really existed. He received no other validation that he was she.

Ben needed to be himself with other people. Therapy was the only place where he expressed his true feelings, that is until he met Jenny.

This woman would have preferred to be a man. She was lesbian and loved women. Ben and Jenny became close friends. Their sexual identity confusion was a common bond. The irony of that relationship was that she craved acceptance as a male from a male, and he wanted acceptance from her for his femininity.

Ben had trouble maintaining relationships. The secret of his sexual identity prevented genuine contact. Many people were attracted by his wit and creativity, which were clearly in the superior range, but his inner self remained elusive. Ben had isolated himself from his family, friends, and work associates. He ached with loneliness, but drove away each person that offered the possibility of a relationship. Never telling the whole truth about himself, only hinting at it in bits and pieces, Ben nevertheless hoped to find acceptance for who he was. This would not happen until he gave up his defenses. There was no way anyone could relate to Ben sexually; he had no stable sexual self to offer. He summarized it by saying, "They are scared off by my weirdness." He did not have the same experience with Jenny.

Ben: Nothing daunts her. She came over to do laundry, her machine was out; I happened to be crossed. She was early, I had planned to change. Even though she knew, I expected the usual shock, disbelief, and disgust. She just walked by, carrying her laundry basket through. All she said was, "Nice sweater, you need some pearls, and your falsies are a little small."

I was struck with the elation he felt. He was so happy just to be accepted. His eyes met mine; no tears, but a lot of moisture. I felt his joy and was profoundly touched. My own eyes teared slightly. There was a bittersweetness to it. The world had withheld so much from Ben because he was different. How tortured his soul must be, to feel such gratitude for simple acceptance.

Jenny continued to give him that and more. She shopped with him when he was fully cross-dressed. They picked out clothes for one another together. His taste was decidedly better than hers. By now I realized she was a former client. I recalled the way she had dressed when she was in therapy sessions with me—like a truck driver. Quite a contrast with Ben's sophistication. I knew she would benefit from his suggestions.

He gave to her in other ways, through stereotypic exchanges that they had never had the opportunity to experience in conventional relationships. He ironed her shirts and cooked soup for her. And she was late for dinner in the masculine way.

Ben: She didn't even call. It's one thing to be twenty minutes late, but an hour and a half! My biscuits were ruined. (His eyes sparkled, belying his words.)

Dr. Doyle (with a very slight inflection, denoting a question): There is something you liked about that?

Ben flushed with pleasure because I understood. It validated him. His self-acceptance and confidence were growing. He had found someone with whom he could be a woman.

And then Jenny fell in love, with a woman. I learned about this development in one of Ben's letters, which he customarily dropped at my office prior to our sessions. That week they also had figured out that I had been Jenny's therapist. So Ben had his choice of two topics to talk about when he came in.

Ben: Why didn't you tell me you were her shrink? (in a reproachful, angry tone as if I had betrayed him).

Dr. Doyle: Ben, you know I don't discuss my clients without their signed consent.

Ben: So you won't admit it, even now.

He was angry with me, but the underlying pain was more significant.

Dr. Doyle: You're hurting, Ben. Tell me about the pain inside.

He threw his briefcase down on the couch and sank to the floor. I sat near him.

Ben (shouting): You knew I was going into this, full-tilt boogie, and didn't warn me. (As if I could predict the future.)

I felt defensive. I wasn't going to acknowledge that Jenny had been my client, nor was I going to explain that I had never been certain it was she.

There was a long wait. He started to breathe more evenly. I

thought he was calming himself. And then suddenly he began to shout again.

Ben: She's gone! The only frigging person in the world who accepted me and she's gone! She's gone! She's gone!

His voice rose to a wail, and he repeated over and over again, "She's gone! She's gone!" until he wore himself out.

His pain was so intense it filled the room. I looked at him and paced my breathing, something I had learned in yoga. I wanted my calmness to flow into him. I continued to breathe audibly. The suggestion took hold. Ben started to breathe with me. Slowly he calmed. Looking at me, he repeated quietly, "She's gone. It's over."

I had an eerie feeling. I was uncertain whether he meant that Jenny was gone or that his inner woman was gone. I did not ask. Then slowly he began to talk about it, to grieve his loss.

Ben: I knew it couldn't last. I've never had that before, someone who knew me and liked me, loved me.

I thought Ben's voice sounded a little flat.

Dr. Doyle: Ben now you know it can happen. You can be loved.

I was a little startled at my own response. I wanted to reframe his thinking. In terms of therapy it was more a gain than a loss. Moreover, I did not want to reinforce his theatrical grieving.

Ben stared at me, furious that I could suggest that his relationship with Jenny was so trivial that it could be replicated. It was clearly something he had not yet considered. He was ready to settle into his grieving, and he wanted me to comfort him. I decided not to do that. His reaction seemed a little exaggerated. Maybe it was Ben's version of a grief-stricken woman. Since he had been conditioned as a man to conceal his feelings, when he did release them they might sound unnatural.

Dr. Doyle: Tell me what you are feeling right now.

Ben: Confused, angry, lost.

Dr. Doyle: Are those feelings coming from your inner self? I want to know more about the woman within. Is she still there?

Ben looked tired. He was leaning against the couch behind him. He had closed his eyes. Opening them, he spoke in a low voice. "I don't know."

Then he closed his eyes and actually fell asleep. I did not disturb him for the remainder of the session, about twenty minutes. I awakened him by touching his arm.

Dr. Doyle: Ben, wake up. You've been asleep and have had a little rest. It is time to go.

Ben: Okay, thanks.

I was unclear about what had happened. He seemed different, calm and even happy.

The experience with Jenny had been significant for Ben. He had felt love and acceptance from her, and short lived though their relationship was, it enabled him to go on to another, this time with a man. It too started as a friendship. Ben cross-dressed from the very beginning, and his new friend accepted it without apparent conflict.

My understanding of Ben's sexuality was incomplete. There appear to be numerous, yet unclassified, sexual identity disorders. This inhibits clinician understanding; mine was no exception. This new male friend of Ben's was content with the designation "gay," but he reportedly did not see himself as homosexual any more than Ben did. We can't call everything denial; what really mattered was that they accepted one another.

Ben: I take a lot of freedom with Hal. I cross and make up when I want to. I don't wait to see if it's a good time for him. My attitude is, take it or leave it, sort of like yours.

I was startled that Ben saw me that way, though of course, he had acquired many of my characteristics and mannerisms in therapy, through incidental learning. I did not see myself as that arrogant. Learning goes both ways.

"You sound cocky," I said. "I like that," reflecting Ben's attitude toward his rapidly expanding self-esteem.

There were other changes. He had resigned his position and started a free-lance business, marketing his creative fabric designs. Although his initial motivation was to make money for the sexual reassignment surgery, he gradually came to revel in his own productivity and success. For the first time he enjoyed what he was doing. He could focus on his work without the constant distraction of his "secret" sexual identity.

Ben's sexual behavior increased. He maintained a monogamous relationship with Hal. He spoke less and less of being trapped in a male body, but he continued to think of himself as a woman, feeling more relaxed when cross-dressed. He continued to develop nonsexual relationships with women. He felt especially good if he was in a group of women and was accepted as "one of the girls." He was unrelenting in his drive to learn about being a woman; how to walk, talk, dress, and accessorize.

Ben: I've missed so much. I'll never get it back (looking forlorn but sounding matter of fact at the same time).

Dr. Doyle: Talk about what you've missed.

Ben: Having my period, using tampons, having a penis inside my vagina. Oral and anal penetration are not the same.

The question of reassignment surgery remained unresolved. Ben could now afford it, but now that he understood himself and the full meaning of sexual identity, genetic and acquired, he doubted that it would work for him.

Ben: There is no surgical intervention that can give me the sense of being a girl and then a woman. The experience of Brownies, Girl Scouts, cheerleading, that first bra, and more, that I have never known.

I knew better than to insert one of my bright cheery little reassurances. I remained silent. It was one of our last sessions. I remember feeling a sense of accomplishment and satisfaction about the work we had done together.

6
Loretta: Incestuous Pedophilia, Nonexclusive Type (DSM-III-R-302.20)

Loretta was beset with repetitive and recurrent sexual urges and fantasies about being in a power position with infant males. She was involuntarily aroused by the thought or sight of infant male genitals. She reported interest in the genitalia of an eighteen-month-old baby boy, her own son. This was nonexclusive pedophilia, in that Loretta could respond with sexual arousal to adult males, but only after prolonged stimulation. Loretta felt her strongest arousal response to women her own age, or older. Like many people with this condition, Loretta had herself been a victim of sexual abuse in childhood. Her father had sexually abused her numerous times. She thinks she was an infant when it started, but she has difficulty remembering back that far.

Most of my work with Loretta was done when she was a young adult, but I had been consulted as a family therapist when Loretta was only a child of ten. She had run away from home sometime after midnight on a very cold night in January. She had walked to the home of her Sunday school teacher, who lived several miles away. The teacher, one of my training associates, had called me because Loretta showed her bruises on her thighs and said her father had touched her genitals and stuck his penis into her. Loretta said she had told her mother but was not believed. Instead she was scolded for making up stories about her father.

Thus began my long, intermittent history of counseling with the family. At first I worked mainly with Loretta and her parents. Our initial goal, after counseling with Loretta, was to comply with child protection laws and get the father out of the home and into therapy. This was done with great difficulty, because Loretta's mother, Rhonda, did not want to acknowledge that anything was wrong. She maintained this position long after the medical and police reports had concluded otherwise. The case was complicated by the fact that Loretta's mother was pregnant at the time the counseling began, and later gave birth to twin girls.

In a family session the mother, Rhonda, spoke bitterly of how hard her life was, trying to care for the infant girls without help from their father.

Rhonda: This isn't fair I'm so tired, why did this have to happen?

She dissolved into tears. Loretta, then almost twelve, was sitting on the floor holding the twins in her arms. She pushed a box of Kleenex across the floor to her mother with her foot.

(my involvement was as a supervisor at the time):

Training associate: You've got your hands full, and it looks like you're trying to take care of Mother, too.

Loretta did not respond. She sat there rocking her sisters, looking fearful.

Training associate: Loretta, do you feel you have to take care of everyone?

Rhonda (breaking in before Loretta could respond): Her? What about me? I'm stuck with all three of them while he gets to do anything he wants. . . . What about me? (dissolving into tears again).

I was touched by Rhonda's anguish. She did have a hard life, and it was unfair. But I was even more concerned about Loretta. She felt guilty, unwanted, and confused. Forced into two unwanted female roles, long before she was able to understand or fulfill them. Forced by her father to be a wife substitute, and in the aftermath, forced to be a mother to her little sisters.

Loretta and her father, mother, and sisters were in and out of therapy with members of my staff and other mental health professionals for years. The family would seek help on a crisis basis only after some kind of sexual abuse had occurred, but would remain in therapy only long enough to satisfy the legal requirements.

After the father, Lee, was somehow permitted to move back into the home, not much time passed before he molested his other two daughters. The child protection services were called in once again.

Loretta's early childhood development had been seriously affected; the damage done to her was extensive. She couldn't trust her father not to use her sexually; she couldn't trust her mother to believe and protect her; and she couldn't trust the authorities, police, or child protection agencies to shield her or her sisters from further sexual abuse.

It's not clear why she decided to come to me for individual counseling years later as a young adult. Perhaps she remembered me as a kindly, if somewhat shadowy, mother figure in the background during those early sessions when she first attempted to escape from her father's sexual assaults.

Loretta: Do you remember me?

Dr. Doyle: Yes.

Loretta: Just to fill you in. Mom and Dad are divorced again, for the third time. The twins are as messed up as I am, and Mom still has her head in the sand. (Sounding very bitter and angry, she continued.) I'm married, have a young son, and I'm in graduate school. I want to be a sex therapist.

She looked at me intently, trying to discern my response. Returning her gaze, I remembered that prepubescent girl trying to care for her sisters, her mother, and herself because there was no one else to do it. I said nothing, so she went on.

Loretta (smiling a little wryly): I know, I'm so messed up, how can I possibly help someone else.

Dr. Doyle (supportively): We don't have to be perfect. We just have to know what our problems are.

Loretta: I've got plenty of problems. All sexual. The rest of my life is okay.

Most of Loretta's feelings about sex were conflicting and confused. They seemed to flood her as she spoke. Thoughts, feelings, and images spilled out, without apparent connection or chronology.

Loretta: I can't enjoy sex. He's always there. Women are more interesting to me, even as a child when I masturbated. I used to be able to with Fred (her spouse). My sisters are still at risk, so is my son. It's sick. I'm not making sense, am I?

Dr. Doyle: Let's start with your feelings. What are you feeling right now? Slowly, we've got plenty of time.

I paced my voice, pronouncing each word deliberately, slowly, and in a low tone. It worked. She slowed down and was able to order her thoughts.

Loretta: I can't enjoy sex with Fred anymore. Before we were married it was great. But now he reminds me of my Dad. He makes me want to vomit. When he's in his business suit, he looks good, even handsome, but when he's undressed or in his undershorts, he makes me sick.

Loretta felt sexually attracted to women and fantasized initiating sex and being very active with them. The issue that concerned her most of all, however, was her intense sexual urges and fantasies about her own son.

Loretta: I'm so afraid I'm going to give in and do something terribly wrong to my own son.

Dr. Doyle: Do you mean sexually abuse him?

Loretta: Yeah, I'd just kill myself if I did, but sometimes when he's asleep and looking so innocent, I feel so attracted to looking at and playing with his penis.

Dr. Doyle: Have you done that?

Loretta: No, but I could have. I'm so afraid I'm like my Dad, afraid, afraid.

She repeated the word several times, face crumpled. She cried for a while, then wiped her eyes with a tissue.

Loretta: I hate it that I'm like him.

Dr. Doyle: You seem motivated to change that.

Loretta obviously drew comfort from my support. She went on to describe her reactions to her son's genitals.

Loretta: They are just so small, so clean. It makes me want to touch him and give him pleasure.

When Loretta said she wanted to "give him pleasure," she was repeating an excuse that I had heard many times before from perpetrators of sex crimes against children. It was clear that she was capable of molesting her son and might already have done so.

Dr. Doyle: How would you feel if you were to do that?

Loretta: Aroused. I feel aroused just talking about it right now.

I remained silent, wanting to encourage Loretta in exploring her feelings, but I didn't want to sanction the inappropriate arousal response toward her son.

Dr. Doyle: Other feelings?

Loretta: Scared, that I'd make him into a crazy person like me and my father.

Dr. Doyle: We do have to teach you how to discriminate sexually.

Loretta: What do you mean?

Dr. Doyle: Many of your sexual feelings and memories run together. Normally, you would respond to age-appropriate people, of the opposite sex. You seem to have an overgeneralized arousal response.

I was not satisfied with my response, too cognitive. Yet Loretta's emotionality had already clouded her thought processes. I wasn't sure how much feeling I could evoke.

Loretta: It's gotten me into a lot of trouble.

Dr. Doyle: I think it would help if we sorted out your sexual responses into present and past, appropriate and inappropriate categories.

Loretta: You mean what's right and what's wrong?

Dr. Doyle: Yes, and also tighten up your thought boundaries so they won't be so fuzzy every time you have a sexual feeling.

We worked on this for about a year. Loretta would report incidents from the past and present relative to her sexual impulses. We set out to establish a definite sexual identity or ideal sexual self for her. She had great difficulty with this. As she recalled and labeled her father's sexual behaviors as totally inappropriate, she compared them to her own sexual impulses toward her son and became aware of a disturbing parallel. At this point, a great deal of hysteria and denial occurred. Loretta would engage in repetitious justifications for her behaviors, citing incident after incident that had happened when she was a child that she believed had "made her the way she was."

Loretta: I could hear him upstairs, going at it with her, and I knew he would pay me a visit sometime later in the night. When I tried to get away, he would hit me. I yelled and cried. I knew everyone could hear, but nobody came.

Loretta was screaming and crying, as if she were reliving those sexual assaults in my office. It was difficult for me to determine whether the catharsis was effective. Was she actually draining away old feelings that had never been expressed, or was this a hysterical denial of responsibility for her current sexual impulses and behaviors? I never knew for sure.

What I did notice was that the successive outbursts gradually diminished, and Loretta could talk, not scream, about what had happened to her. She also reported less frequent fantasies about her son's genitalia.

With anguish in her voice, Loretta talked about how everything had returned to "normal" about a year after our initial family intervention, even though her father had experienced a year of group therapy. Her father returned to the home and continued to visit her at night. She gave up trying to resist and just accepted his advances. After she no longer resisted him, he was less abusive. She never let herself move or make any sounds during those forced sexual encounters; she closed her eyes and wanted it to be over.

The overgeneralization was clear. Those repeated incestuous assaults had had the effect of destroying her capacity to respond normally in later years, during sexual encounters with her husband. She could not discriminate present from past. In sexual encounters, Loretta frequently rejected her husband and held herself back from feeling any physical pleasure, just as she used to hide her reactions to her father's stimulation of her genitals even though it felt pleasurable. She made no sound or movement that would betray her enjoyment.

Although she hated sexual encounters, she loved to tease her husband and other males by the way she postured herself. It gave her a sense of power and control to be able to excite men, but not to satisfy them. This was somewhat similar to what she felt when she had sexual impulses toward her infant son. These behaviors were directly related to her childhood experience. Overgeneralization had created a ripple effect; all sexual sensations, thoughts, and images were distorted. Loretta's psychosexual disorder resulted not just from the initial sexual trauma that occurred when she was molested by her father, but from the multiple effects of that occurrence. The longer she remained untreated, the more entrenched her disorder became.

Her defensive reactions, conscious as well as unconscious, were designed to protect her from the recurrence of those terrifying sexual episodes. For example, her arousal feelings toward women were designed to distract her from being aroused with men. This would keep her from getting into sexual encounters with males, where she knew she would feel exploited and abused. Similarly, her intense arousal feelings and fantasies about sexually abusing infants and small children gave her the opportunity to be the exploiter rather than the exploited. These defenses, based on imperfect learning, were not effective. They did not relieve Loretta from the fear and anxiety she felt around all things sexual; instead, they generated feelings of confusion and guilt. The resultant pathology rendered her potentially dangerous to herself and others.

Initially Loretta's defensiveness led her to conceal the extent of her pathology from me. She omitted telling me about a series of incidents in which she had, as a teenager, sexually abused her infant sisters.

Loretta: I don't know how to tell you this. You are going to hate me. I hate myself; what I've done is terrible.

She seemed to be winding herself up to waste half of our session in still another defensive maneuver. Overstatement, exaggeration, anything to keep herself from feeling the anxiety of further disclosure. I wasn't in the mood for it.

Dr. Doyle (interrupting her in a low, steady reassuring tone): It's okay, Loretta, just tell me. Let's trust ourselves to work it out.

Loretta: When my baby sisters were small . . . (looking at me and then away) I, uh . . . when I was changing their diapers . . . I would . . . (her voice dropped off).

I felt queasy inside. There was something especially foreboding about the way Loretta was struggling with her words and feelings. I just sat there waiting. She turned her body sideways, so she did not have to look at my face and I could not see hers.

Loretta (continuing): I used to lick them. I mean like an animal. . . . Instead of washing their little bottoms, I licked them like an animal. He did that to me, he did that to me!!

She seemed to be offering half apology or excuse, half explanation for her behavior.

She started to make dry, heaving sounds, coughed a little, and then vomited all over my Oriental rug. I was appalled, and so was Loretta. She started to cry. She shook with humiliation and shame. Low, gurgling sounds came out between the sobs. She slid to the floor, sitting in her vomit, letting it ooze between her fingers. I knew she was distracting herself from the acute pain of her degradation by wallowing in it.

I had my own feelings to deal with. Sometimes I have a weak stomach. I was fighting a complementary response. I couldn't let myself vomit. She would misinterpret it as disgust and rejection of her. With great effort, I forced myself to concentrate on what she was feeling inside so that I could respond to her and make therapeutic use of her emotional state. Moving my chair close, I put my hand on her shoulder. She reached up and touched my hand and held on. Her fingers were wet; the smell from her vomit permeated the room. She said, "I'm sorry, I'm sorry."

The anguish in her voice distracted me from all else. I was on track. I could work again.

Dr. Doyle: This is a good thing that has happened here. (She looked up at me in disbelief.) You have vomited up the remainder of your past. You can heal now.

She believed it, so did I. In subsequent sessions, Loretta talked about how her father would lick her genitals and tell her that they were "animals," that "we were all animals." It had been a horrifying and degrading experience for her. She had tried to erase it from mind and memory by taking on his role with her sisters. In the role of the perpetrator, she hoped that by reversing positions she could erase the unbearable feeling of victimization.

This didn't work; it only added to her guilt and confusion. Loretta repeated this behavior with her twin sisters until just before they started to talk. She stopped because she was afraid she would be found out, but whenever she babysat, and when she had her own son, she experienced persistent sexual impulses to repeat the behavior. Earlier in treatment, Loretta had agreed to tell her husband about the impulses and work out a child care schedule that would safeguard her son. She also agreed not to put herself in situations in which she had an opportunity to look at or fondle her son's genitals.

Concurrently, we tried to recondition her arousal response to her husband. I met with them both, and we worked out a plan together. He agreed to wear after-shave lotion and cologne, and to do anything else he could to be "different" from Loretta's father. This included wearing colorful briefs that they shopped for together, and having sexual encounters in daylight or with the lights on. Sexual encounters no longer took place in bed, as they always had when Loretta's father molested her. In summary, we did everything we could to alter the conditions under which their sexual encounters occurred so that they would be very different from the assault encounters Loretta had experienced with her father.

This rational, matter-of-fact behavioral approach to the different components of Loretta's sexual problems worked well. The hardest thing for Loretta was to comply with my request to initiate sexual encounters with her husband, in which she aroused and satisfied him. She felt she was giving in to him and "being bad." I explained to her over and over again that she had a great deal of power in these encounters to be "good" and "do it right," that she was making love with her husband, not being molested by her father. In return, I assured her, she would receive exciting stimulation and satisfaction. Most of all, I stressed that these behaviors were wholesome and appropriate within the confines of a marital relationship.

This was a re-parenting approach that involved elements of regression. At times, Loretta became my child, and accepted me as a role model. Utilizing the transference was an integral part of therapy. Because of the normal feelings of caring for and dependence that arise within the client for the therapist, I had an opportunity to "layer in" clear, appropriate sexual boundaries.

Initially, Loretta's sexual response was both overgeneralized and inhibited. She responded with arousal to both males and females, as well as infants and adults. She also had genital sensations whenever anyone showed caring and/or interest in her. Generally, when she had these feelings, she inhibited them and trained herself not to respond. As she began to trust me and see me as a significant force in her life, she developed a genital response to me. She experienced feelings of sexual arousal during our sessions or when she thought of me. She had fantasies about developing a personal relationship with me. Between sessions she would often write about these feelings, but was too embarrassed to talk about them in session. I encouraged her to talk about the sexual feelings she had and explained how I saw them. Even though she was disappointed that I did not have the same type of feelings for her, she gradually came to accept her feelings of desire as okay, and seemed proud of the fact that she did not try to act them out with me. These feelings then occurred less frequently, because the boundaries between us were very clear. This gave Loretta an experience wherein she was not sexually exploited by someone in power for whom she had strong feelings. At the same time, she learned not to exploit anyone over whom she herself had power. This curative experience contrasted with Loretta's earlier associations with sexual power and exploitation.

Loretta's therapy moved slowly. We met on a weekly basis for more than eighteen months before she began to show real consolidation of the changes she was making.

She managed to transfer more of her arousal feelings to her husband. We had several conjoint sessions in which it became clear that he was angry with her for the expense of therapy, as well as for her problems with responding sexually to him. Although he was generally supportive of her, his anger came out as inattentiveness to her feelings and to the relationship. For example, he would stay up late, watching television for hours after she had gone to bed. He complained that they did not have enough sex, but did little to create opportunities for closeness that might develop into sexual intimacy. As we talked about this in conjoint sessions, he expressed and integrated his anger. Both he and Loretta were able to see how their sexual relationship could be altered. Loretta and her husband, Fred, expressed themselves humorously to help overcome their embarrassment at talking about explicit sexual behaviors. This carried over to their interactions at home, and they became more playful in general, which greatly enhanced their sexual encounters.

Loretta still was seriously hampered by unresolved feelings toward her mother.

Loretta: I feel guilty, like I took something from her, something she wanted and needed more than I did.

I did not respond. I knew that Loretta had been reassured in previous therapy with me and other mental health professionals that a child is not responsible for the sexual behavior of adults. She also knew this from her training as a sex therapist. She went on.

Loretta: I teased him. I egged him on. . . . Sometimes . . . never when we were in bed, but sometimes in the car when mom was there, I'd pull my skirt up or do something just to let them know that I was thinking about it. (A tear slid down her cheek.) I wish I hadn't done that.

I said nothing. She went on to talk about her great need to feel loved by her mother.

Loretta: She was always there when I came home from school, with a snack she knew I would like . . . but she never hugged me or kissed me, nothing. (Her voice faltered.) Sometimes I think that's why I want, wanted to be with a woman so bad.

Dr. Doyle: Those feelings are still there?

Loretta: Sometimes. (She smiled reassuringly.) I know better, but I would like to have a session with my parents.

I nodded yes. This was toward the end of our work together. I think Loretta was seeking closure in terms of her own therapy with me as well as with her past sexual experiences.

It was hard for Loretta to persuade her parents to come to a session. They were in ongoing family therapy with Loretta's sisters and did not welcome what they thought of as another intrusion into their "business." But they did come. At the beginning of the session I asked them all to state their goals for the time we had together.

Lee (Loretta's father, still acting as head of the family): To lay it to rest, to get it over with.

Rhonda (Loretta's mother, nodding in agreement, sitting very close to her husband and holding onto his arm): To help her (nodding in Loretta's direction).

Dr. Doyle (to Rhonda): You've got as much of a right to want something for yourself as the others do.

I was trying to touch Rhonda, to empower her, so she would dare to be present as a real person, not just a rough approximation of the wife and mother role. She looked at me, perhaps softening a bit, and then her eyes narrowed suspiciously.

Rhonda: I know what I've done wrong, you don't have to tell me.

Her eyes looked tired. She looked so worn. I hoped that she was benefitting from her therapy.

Loretta spoke next, without waiting for further acknowledgment from me as she usually did. I felt excitement. Loretta was taking over the session.

Loretta: I want it to be over too. It is over for me. (She was smiling. We all looked at her in surprise.) I'm better, better than I've ever been. (She looked at her father.) I can't hate you any more. . . . I know from what happened to me and what I've learned in therapy that you were messed up as a kid and were just acting out your frustrations on me. (She turned to her mother.) You did the best you could, you just don't know any better.

She went over to the couch where they were sitting and knelt in front of them. She reached for their hands and said, "You are my parents. I love you."

I was stunned. Is this what I had taught her? It didn't seem real—too theatrical, too sweet, too everything. I pulled myself out of my own reaction and focused on my clients. Loretta's parents sat there motionless, like little wooden figures, their daughter kneeling before them with tears streaming down her face. Would they respond? Rhonda, the mother, placed her hand on Loretta's head but said nothing. Lee looked at Loretta and then at his wife. Was there moisture in his eyes?

Dr. Doyle: What is it that you're feeling, Lee?

Lee: Forgiven.

I looked at Loretta. She was looking at me as a cotherapist would. I knew that this was her way of terminating therapy with me as well as obtaining closure with her parents. I also knew that there was a lot of pain left inside of her, and anger, but she was choosing not to focus on that. Letting go of her anger would help her to integrate the whole sexual abuse issue.

That was my final session with Loretta. She wanted it that way. I would have preferred one more, to process and consolidate the family session, perhaps for my own benefit. But Loretta had taken control of her own life. What further processing she did, she did without me, and that was good.

7
Frank: Ego Dystonic Homosexuality and Sexual Disorder Not Otherwise Specified (DSM-III-R-302.00; DSM-III-R-302.90)

Frank was persistently distressed about his sexual orientation. He was sexually aroused by males. His fantasies and dreams were almost exclusively of males. Many of his sexual experiences, especially his early ones, had been with males. But he did not want to be homosexual, and he refused to use that term when referring to himself. The closest he came to it was "bisexual." Distress about his sexual orientation had led him to develop a pattern of sexual conquests involving a succession of women, and to a lesser degree men, who existed only as things or objects to be used.

Frank: I'm not gay. Fags are attracted to me, but so are women. I get hit on everywhere I go.

He was middle-aged, but he sounded like, and dressed like, an adolescent, preoccupied with the way he looked sexually. The first time I saw Frank he was wearing tight, faded jeans and a polo shirt. His crotch area bulged, making it look as though his genitals were enormous. I was later to learn that he stuffed cotton and tissue into his jockstrap to achieve that effect.

Frank was a reluctant client. He had been caught in a surprise urine analysis at his place of employment. He was given the option of using the company psychologist or seeking counseling from an outside clinician. He got my name from a woman with whom he was having an extramarital affair.

He was alcoholic and drank on a daily basis after he finished working, vodka mixed with anything. He even poured it into coke cans and soft drink bottles to hide what he was drinking.

He was quick to deny that drinking was a problem. His main concern, he said, was a desire to increase his heterosexual arousal. His sexual response to women was very weak. He could get and maintain an erection only if his genitals were directly stimulated by his sex partner or by himself. When he attempted penetration vaginally or anally with a woman, he would frequently lose his erection. He recovered the situation by giving oral sex, so that his partner would be satisfied. His erectile response was functionally similar with males. Although he would get spontaneous erections without direct stimulation with males, when he attempted anal penetration, his erections would usually go soft. He would offer oral sex as a compensatory measure, but he seemed much more distressed when this happened with a male than with a female. Women, he thought, were more understanding and accepting.

The woman he had married, and with whom he had an eleven-year-old son, had apparently run out of understanding and acceptance. Several weeks prior to the time when Frank was caught in the drug screen, she had taken their son and left the state. She was now filing for divorce and custody of their son.

None of this seemed to bother Frank. All he wanted to talk about was his sexual arousal response.

Frank: What would I have to do to keep it up with a woman? I've tried everything I can think of, including thinking about men when we're fucking. Nothing works.

Dr. Doyle: Have you tried accepting yourself as a homosexual?

He sprang up from the couch angrily, almost knocking me backward off my chair.

Frank: I told you. I'm not gay!!!

Silence. I needed a few moments to compose myself. I looked at him and pointed back to the spot on the couch where he had been sitting. He sat down.

Dr. Doyle (in a low voice): You sure don't want to be gay.

Frank: I've fought it all my life and you're not going to talk me into it now.

Silence again. I just looked at him and sighed. He got up again. I thought he was going to leave. Instead, he walked around my chair and stood behind me. I was scared, but I just sat there looking at the clock. The second hand slowly moved around several times. Was he going to break my neck?

To ease the tension, I got up slowly and quietly walked to the couch where he had been and sat down.

Dr. Doyle: Sit down, Frank. Let's talk.

He sat down in my chair. I felt relieved. It wasn't the first time I had felt fear in the presence of a client, but this time there was an eerie quality permeating the atmosphere of the room, as if Frank's anxiety and fear were flitting from point to point without settling on anything, internally or externally. He seemed to feel better sitting in my chair.

Frank: Sorry I'm so fucked up, Doc.

I looked at him with a light nod of yes.

Dr. Doyle: You hate everything about "gay," don't you? (I didn't want to risk saying he was gay, but I had to get him on track somehow.)

Frank: I don't like men. I've hated every man I've been with. (He laughed.) Not that I've loved the women.

Dr. Doyle: It's hard to love anyone when you don't love yourself.

He looked at me, shook his head sideways and lapsed into silence. Loving himself had never occurred to him.

I waited. I couldn't see the clock because it was behind me. Then he said, "You don't like me, do you?" I was surprised. Was it true? I wasn't sure how I felt about him. I didn't like what was happening, and that is what I said.

Dr. Doyle: I don't like what's happening.

Frank: You're used to being in control, aren't you? (laughing again).

Dr. Doyle: We're wasting time, Frank. I can't see the clock. I think our time is up.

I got up, walked to my desk and picked up my appointment book.

Dr. Doyle: Do you want to reschedule?

Frank: Yeah.

Dr. Doyle: I can meet with you next Tuesday at three. (I wasn't making it easy for him, that was not a good time. I wanted to add, "take it or leave it," but I didn't. Instead, I recited my litany.) If you have to cancel, I need twenty-four hours' notice or you are charged for the time. My fee is $90. I need a check for today's session.

Frank: I know. Mitze told me the drill, cash on the barrel head. (He threw down his check and strode out.) See you next week.

It was clear that anger was his favored response. The smallest stress seemed to evoke it. I don't like anger. It makes me feel like fighting — not very helpful in a therapy session. I have to compensate for my anger and the impact it has on my ability to be effective. Compensatory behaviors don't have to be subtle, as long as they get the job done. My robotic little recitation, "If you have to cancel, I need twenty-four hours' notice or you get charged for the time," falls into the category of bracketing my anger. Frank knew he was being hit. I had put him in his place. If he wanted to work with me, it would be on my terms. Once that was settled, we did okay. In fact, Frank probably couldn't have trusted me to guide him until he knew I could play hardball.

Which of his many issues should we focus on? Frank's drinking was a problem, and so was his erectile response. The effect alcohol was having on his erectile response was unclear. I wondered if he could maintain an erection with a man or a woman, since he was so anxious about being homosexual. Actually, his erectile response was not the primary issue, and although he had been referred for an alcohol problem, his sexual identity confusion was the main source of his anxiety. He rarely approached a man or a woman without having had something to drink. It seemed that just being sexual made him anxious and confused. Was he dangerous? He had lost control of his anger with me; was that a sample of his behavior?

Homophobia had seriously damaged Frank's sexual self-esteem. By the time he was fourteen, he had feared he was homosexual. He had already internalized extremely negative feelings about homosexuality. He didn't want to hate himself, but society was telling him that if he felt sexually attracted to males he was despicable. He concluded that his best alternative was to deny the feelings. As is often the case, this blunted his sensitivity to all his feelings except anger and fear. Warm feelings of love did not enter his awareness. He had never been able to enjoy the sensual and erotic feelings associated with masturbation or sexual encounter without feeling intense guilt and shame.

Working with him was very difficult. He needed more self-awareness. There were many unresolved feelings to be integrated. Many incidents relative to his sexual development had to be explored. But Frank could not talk about his sexual orientation for very long without becoming defensive. He couldn't tolerate the fear that built as he moved toward the inevitable. He sensed that talking about it made it more real.

He needed continual encouragement and reassurance.

Dr. Doyle: It will help to talk about your sexual orientation. You'll feel calmer.

No response. Minutes passed. He sat there staring at me, looking stressed. I didn't want the anxiety to build; he didn't need more than he was already experiencing. So I broke the silence.

Dr. Doyle (in a low monotone): Just whenever you're ready, Frank. (I was pacifying his fear; I was babying him. It worked; he spoke.)

Frank: Does this run in families?

Dr. Doyle: Sometimes. (I looked at him and nodded slightly.)

Frank: I think there were some queers on my mother's side of my family. My dad and uncle used to make snide remarks about Mother's older brother, who was never married or had any girlfriends. He was beaten up coming out of a gay bar. Stupid asshole should have known better.

I was struck with how consistent his hostility was. Choicepoint. I didn't want to reinforce his gay bashing by listening to it, but he needed to express both sides of his conflict in order to continue. I remained silent.

Frank: Poor bastard, he drank more than I do. He didn't have a chance.

Dr. Doyle: You sound as if he's dead.

Frank: Yeah. He killed himself. None of us went to the funeral, not even my mother.

There was a change in his voice tone. The death of his gay uncle was obviously significant.

Frank had been nine years old when that happened. He didn't remember there being much talk in the family about it. It had scared him. And because no one talked about it, the fear remained encapsulated within him. It contributed to the associated fear around anything to do with homosexuality. That fear inhibited his ability to discriminate between past and present, himself and others. As he became more aware of his sexual reactions and realized he wasn't like other boys, he feared he too would kill himself. He didn't realize he had a choice about how he handled his sexual identity, and he exaggerated the danger of being gay.

During one of our early exploration sessions, Frank became so frightened that he would hurt himself that he turned his anger and self-hatred toward me for making him look past his denial.

Frank: Why the hell are we talking about this shit? You're going to turn me into a fag. Is that what you want? Are you a fag hag?

By this time he was yelling. His face was contorted, his arms gesturing.

I thought his anger had to be expressed, but I didn't want him to lose control.

Dr. Doyle (in a very low voice): It's okay, Frank, you need to get that feeling out.

I thought I might as well give him permission to vent his anger. Telling him to control himself wouldn't work, but I could make him think about it. He stared at me in disbelief.

Frank: You want me to hit you?

Dr. Doyle: No, Frank. I don't want you to hurt me or you. I just want you to accept yourself. But I am worried about your temper. If we're going to continue to explore your feelings, you might have to go on a medication so you won't get so agitated. What do you think? (I continued to treat him as if he could control himself, even though I wasn't certain that he could.)

Frank: I can't believe you. I just can't believe you. I'm about to bash your face in and you suggest medication. (Shaking his head, he turned around and sat down on the couch.)

Perhaps he felt he had to be the responsible one. Or perhaps the paradox in my intervention had stopped him. Frank couldn't believe me; I couldn't believe myself.

I should have referred Frank to our staff psychiatrist for medication much earlier in therapy. There were signs that his self-hatred and rage were powerful enough to warrant such a referral.

Frank did go on medication. I was surprised at how willingly he did so. In retrospect, I wondered if his angry outburst and my acceptance of it were sufficient to constitute the catharses he needed. As always, I felt a need for more clarity in the mystery of therapy.

The course of therapy changed after that. Frank talked openly about being gay. He did not want to join a subculture. He would never "come out" because it would jeopardize his job security. He was not a limp-wristed flamer. But as he argued against it, his anger and fear diminished.

Something else was happening. Frank was becoming more responsible, less like an adolescent. His brand of macho mellowed. He appeared to have stopped stuffing his jockstrap with tissue paper. His drinking also tapered off. He felt more control, and as a result, his self-esteem increased.

We had been working together for almost a year, meeting on a weekly basis with very few exceptions, when his divorce became final. I asked him to talk about his ex-wife and son. There was little or no emotion in his voice.

Frank: It was a mistake. I married for the wrong reasons. She was pretty enough, but she never turned me on, more like a sister or a mother—no, a stranger. I didn't know her and she didn't know me.

Dr. Doyle: That's sad. (More of a suggestion than anything else.)

Frank looked at me. He didn't understand. He couldn't feel compassion. He had never permitted himself a full range of feelings. His long-standing denial, adopted as a boy, had shielded him from his homosexual identity. It had also blocked the development of normal human emotions people usually feel in relationships. All of his sexual partners, male and female, had meant nothing to him, and neither had his wife and son. They were not real people to him because he had not been a real person with them. The only genuine emotions Frank had known were those he had experienced in therapy. How could I expand that learning?

Dr. Doyle: Frank, how do you feel about me?

He looked at me for a long time. He swallowed, and then looked away. He was uncomfortable.

Frank: You know more about me than anyone else.

(I nodded, smiling a little bit. He continued.)

Frank: I love you. I need you to help me through this.

Dr. Doyle: I want to help you through this and I want to teach you how to feel.

It wasn't clear to me what Frank meant by "this," and I'm sure it wasn't clear to him what I meant by "feel." Cognition is rarely as important as affect in the process of therapy. The love Frank felt, and his open acknowledgment of it, signaled a change. Frank now had access to a full range of feeling, which had to be consolidated before it could be generalized to an outside relationship.

Frank needed some contacts in the gay community. He had never gone to a gay bar. Was it linked to his uncle's tragic experience? The males Frank had sexualized with in the past had approached him in shopping malls and hotel lobbies. He had always been drunk, or near drunk, during the encounters, and he had felt little except for initial arousal. After that, anxiety was the predominant feeling. Either because of what had happened to his uncle, or from the fact that Frank was drinking Coke and Perrier these days, he decided not to attempt the gay bar scene. He went to a few meetings at a gay church, but decided he didn't fit in there either. He wanted me to rescue him.

Frank: Introduce me to some of your other gay clients.

(I had been asked to do this before by other clients.)

Dr. Doyle: No, Frank. I don't do that. It just doesn't feel right to me.

Frank: Shit! Why not?

I didn't feel like arguing, so I said nothing. I didn't have more to say. It didn't feel right for me to introduce my clients to each other; this was true whether they were homosexual or heterosexual. It was more responsibility than I wanted. I don't even fix up my friends.

Frank was disgusted with me. He missed his next session, something he had never done before. I was worried. He had made a lot of progress, but he wasn't quite ready to quit. Or was he? Maybe he had gotten everything he could from therapy.

About three weeks later, he called the office. He had been drinking and wanted to see me. I told him to come in the next day at four o'clock, after the effects of the alcohol had dissipated.

Frank: I blew it.

I just looked at him, waiting. He got up and walked around the room. I remembered his hostility in earlier sessions, but I wasn't afraid this time.

Frank: I had a few drinks and tricked out, but I wasn't drunk. (He looked at me, needing encouragement to go on.)

Dr. Doyle: Talk about it.

Frank: It was different. I felt something. I stayed hard . . . well, almost. He gave me head.

Frank was happy. Proud of himself. He wanted my approval. I had to be careful. I didn't want to jeopardize his self-acceptance, but I didn't approve of the drinking and I didn't know if he had used a condom, even though we had talked about safe sex. I remained silent.

Frank: I'm not going back to the bar.

I wondered if he had sensed my ambivalence. I said nothing.

Frank: I had to prove that I could.

Dr. Doyle: You didn't get beaten up.

Frank (grinning): No.

I saw Frank several times during the next few months. He had been attending some gay AA meetings and had started to establish a group of friends. I was glad he could accept himself and feel happiness.

A note about therapy. Frank's overuse of denial had prevented him from bonding with another person. In the acceptance that he experienced in therapy, Frank had disclosed fears and longings deep within himself. That process generates intense feelings of attachment and affection. Frank's statement, "I love you," expressed a birth of the emotion he had repressed since he was a boy. This marked the beginning of Frank's ability to feel a full range of human emotions. Acceptance, an unknown concept for Frank, provoked him to accept, like, and then love himself.

8
Julie: Gender Identity Disorder of Adolescence or Adulthood Nontranssexual (GIDAANT) (DSM-III-R-302.02)

Julie was afraid to be a woman. She dressed in shapeless, mannish clothing to conceal her body. She had started doing this when she was a teenager. Although her adult sexual history included genital encounters with both men and women, her arousal response was definitely heterosexual. Her discomfort with her genitals was predicated on the fear that as a female she was vulnerable, not only to sexual assault, but to ridicule and abuse as well.

Her psychosexual disorder had its roots in confused childish perceptions of what men and women are supposed to be. Her father was an abusive alcoholic; her mother was a stereotypic ineffectual woman, who took refuge in female role behavior to protect herself from her husband. Neither were acceptable role models for Julie.

As a child, Julie had witnessed repeated situations in which her father berated her mother for not cleaning the house or not preparing food appropriately. He would ridicule her mother's efforts to "do it right" or to please him, and he would curse, push, and slap her. These incidents usually ended with him leaving the house and being gone for several hours, frequently all night. Julie remembered hearing her mother pleading with him not to go.

Recalling one time when her parents were naked, she witnessed an argument and subsequent struggle in the hallway outside their bedroom. It was the first time Julie had seen the contrast in male and female genitalia. She reported taking off her clothing also and looking at her genitals. She was extremely distressed to discover that she did not have a penis like her father.

Julie was disgusted with her mother's behavior. She believed that if her mother would fight back, her father would be more manageable.

Julie had clearly achieved some identification with her mother prior to pubescence. Until that time she had accepted being a girl, enjoyed feminine clothing, played with dolls, and did all the things little girls were expected to do. She continued, however, to be distressed about her genitals. She would try to urinate standing over the toilet, as she knew her father did. She usually did this during or immediately after her parents fought. At this point, she sought male identification in order to relieve her anxiety and fear that she would experience the same treatment as her mother.

By the time she started seventh grade, she began to experience a strong, persistent uneasiness with being a girl.

Julie: I had long hair and boys noticed me. I liked the attention, but my father also started paying more attention to me about the same time.

She stopped speaking and looked at her watch and then at me. Her eyes were dull, as was her general appearance. Stocky in build, devoid of makeup, she was not an attractive person. It was hard to imagine anyone being sexually interested in her.

Dr. Doyle: You stopped in mid-sentence. Something about what you were saying made you uncomfortable.

Julie: I forgot what I was going to say. I have trouble concentrating.

Julie was a substance abuse counselor, referred to me by the clinical director of the agency in which she was employed. She had an undergraduate degree in psychology and was working on her master's degree at the time our sessions began.

She had been diagnosed as depressed and was taking medication. Julie was socially withdrawn and functioning at a very low level professionally. She rarely spoke in staff meetings, failed to do her paperwork, and frequently called in sick. She had been in therapy several times before, but her sexual identity issue had never been addressed. I wondered why. She presented a dyke-like appearance. Her demeanor toward me was not quite that of a boy, not quite that of a girl, rather a combination of both genders, similar to a junior or senior high school boy in heat. She sat like a male, her legs spread apart, rather than crossed in the feminine way.

She told me she liked me and that I was really pretty. Julie would glance at my bustline, and then to my eyes. It was as if she wanted me to think she was interested in me sexually. At first I thought this was a distraction; it did not seem genuine to me. I decided to disclose my reaction.

Dr. Doyle: There's something odd about the sexual messages you are giving off.

She looked at me with interest. Her eyes were no longer dull. I continued.

Dr. Doyle: You sound like you are coming on to me. Are you feeling something sexually?

She blushed. I had startled and embarrassed her. I wondered if I had overplayed my hand. I had evoked a lot of feeling in her. How would she respond?

Julie: I don't have sexual feelings. I'm odd, like you said. How did you know?

I didn't really understand what she was alluding to. How did I know what? I didn't want to lose touch with whatever it was she was feeling. If I said too much, or asked for clarification, I might lead her into more of a thinking than a feeling state.

I stood up and motioned her toward the large, wood-framed mirror that hung in my office.

Dr. Doyle (in a low, hushed tone): What do you see?

Julie stared at herself in the mirror. She looked at her hair and her face; her eyes moved down her body. She was not wearing a bra, and the contours of her breasts were barely perceptible. She turned around and looked at herself from behind. She was wearing jeans and a man's sport shirt. It wasn't tucked in, and it covered her hips. There was no feminine roundness in sight. She looked asexual, a little on the masculine side. She smiled, and sighed. It was obvious that she felt reassured.

I was somewhat puzzled. Why would she engage in come-on behavior with me? She had told me previously she did not respond sexually to women, her arousal response was heterosexual. Had she forgotten that I knew that? I said nothing, but watched for similar behavior.

The lesbian relationships she had been in had not lasted, because Julie would not permit her partners to touch or pleasure her sexually. Sexual activity gradually died out as the other women became bored with the limited sexual expression they were permitted to have with Julie. This was just part of her overall sexual defensiveness.

Whenever she became anxious, whatever the cause, she seemed to take on some sort of masculine identification. It made her feel less vulnerable. She had overgeneralized sexual fear, and anytime she felt anxious, she retreated into masculine identification. She had never divested herself entirely of her feminine identity, however. Julie had a habit of indiscriminately throwing up a smoke screen of confused sexual signals, sometimes with bizarre timing. My impression was of an impersonation of a male, with ultra-feminine highlights.

I asked Julie to tell me about her previous counseling experiences. Her file at work had little or nothing in it, other than the fact that she was an alcoholic in recovery. This is common for staff clinicians in the field of chemical dependency. I asked her about her previous diagnosis of depression. When had she received it? Who had prescribed her medication? Simple data-gathering questions, and yet Julie seemed anxious. She looked like a pathetic, frightened child sitting on the couch. First male, legs spread apart, then female, one leg poised seductively to show the roundness of her hip and thigh. I glimpsed, for the first time, a deep, aching pain in her eyes. Then she spoke. Her voice was high-pitched, measured, and strangely feminine.

Julie: It was a long time ago, out of state. I told the psychiatrist at Centerdale that I needed a refill. He has been signing off on it ever since. We have a working relationship. He sees some of my clients that have a dual diagnosis. (She looked down and then at her watch.)

I felt uncomfortable and a little angry. Internally, I questioned the ethics of the physician who had prescribed her medication under such lax conditions. I reminded myself that everything heard in session is hearsay—a good reason not to focus on content. My mind wandered. I also questioned Julie's choice of counseling as a career. Had she, like so many others in the mental health field, joined our ranks in the hope of clearing up her own confusion? Irrelevant, I concluded. I couldn't suspend therapy to resolve these issues; there would be no payoff in the answers. I needed to get back on track.

Dr. Doyle: Julie, I'm not following you. What you've told me so far doesn't hang together. Help me fill in the blanks.

She looked at me. Her eyes were bright. I knew we were in contact. She was giving me her full attention. She was deciding how much to tell me, how much she trusted me.

Julie: I'm a convicted felon. I tried to kill a man in a barroom fight. He lived. I served two years in a penitentiary before being paroled. I was drunk.

The man had called her a bitch and pushed Julie aside at the bar to order a drink. She had doubled up her fists and hit him repeatedly in the face, catching him by surprise. She knocked him down, jumped on him, and beat his head against the floor. She then took out a switchblade and stabbed him. The police arrived. She was handcuffed and taken to jail. Julie remembered cussing at the police officers, calling them "cocksuckers" and daring them to take her cuffs off so she could "beat their ass."

She looked at me, waiting for my reaction.

Dr. Doyle: That's the sort of thing a man would do. You are a woman.

Julie: I was drunk. I fight a lot when I'm drunk.

Dr. Doyle: Like your father?

Julie (nodding): Yes.

Our time was up. We scheduled our next appointment and she left. I was pleased with our progress. She had trusted me. I had accepted her and had linked her homicidal behavior to the confused identification she had with her father.

It was time to move to the playroom. I wanted to go back to the time when Julie had accepted herself as a little girl. Before doing that, however, I referred her to our staff psychiatrist to be sure her medication was appropriate. It was, and we proceeded.

We began a process of light regression therapy. Julie was encouraged to recall childhood feelings and events that related to her sexual development. The playroom, simply furnished as it was, served as a backdrop to the process of recollection. The toys in the room were generic in nature. That, combined with the positive value of the transference, created an atmosphere for Julie wherein she could relive some of her childhood experiences, this time with a female role model that she could respect and accept. This contrasted with the feelings she had about her mother.

I wanted her to reclaim her femininity and let go of the masculine identity she was using to shield herself from being a woman. The therapeutic process leaned heavily on suggestion and symbolism. I was clear with Julie about our goal and why we were now meeting in the playroom instead of in my office. She was guarded but fascinated, soon becoming immersed in the process. We would sit in beanbags and talk or sit at a small, child-sized table to draw or work with clay. At first she was essentially nonresponsive, showing little interest in the toys except for a black plastic gun and a gray rubber knife, which she liked to hold while we talked. This choice of toys symbolized her defensiveness and masculine identification, providing the needed reassurance.

I asked her to draw a picture of herself as a little girl. At first she sat and stared at the crayons and paper, saying she couldn't draw and didn't know what to do. Supportively, I urged her to try harder. I showed her how, by drawing stick figures of myself and her in the playroom (Figure 1). Finally, she picked up a black crayon and drew a picture of herself lying on a bed with another figure hovering over her (Figure 2). Very slowly, and without expression, she described to me how her father had sexually molested her.

Julie: He just came into my room. Mom was at work. He put his hand under the covers and started to finger me. I tried to pull away . . .

She stopped talking and stared at the beanbag on which she was sitting. There were no tears. She was disassociating herself from what had occurred. Was she feeling anything?

Dr. Doyle (leaning forward and touching her wrist, speaking softly): Say what you are feeling, Julie.

Julie: Nothing. I don't know. It was like that. I felt nothing.

Dr. Doyle: I wonder if it felt good or if it hurt? (I tried to nudge her back to her feelings.)

Figure 1
Lead Drawing for Julie

Figure 2
Julie and Father

Julie: I felt nothing.

(It sounded true, not like a denial.)

Dr. Doyle: I wonder how it affected you.

(She was silent, then spoke after quite some time.)

Julie: I don't know.

We had just a little time left, about seven minutes. I wanted her to think about the questions I had asked; about how it felt and the impact it had on her.

Dr. Doyle: Let's write down the parts of that experience we want to know more about.

Picking up the black crayon, Julie wrote in a large hand, "Did it hurt? Did it feel good?" Her response was not complete, but some consolidation had occurred.

Dr. Doyle: Good. Now let's stretch.

I stretched and yawned and tried to loosen up my body. It was a graceful movement I had learned in yoga. Julie did the same. In fact, she stretched and yawned in exactly the same way I did. There was no attempt on her part to posture herself in a masculine way. I was using the stretching movements to encourage grace and femininity.

In subsequent sessions we explored the sexual molestation. Julie talked about how it had affected her. We always started with drawing materials. Julie always selected a black crayon.

Dr. Doyle: You always use black, Julie. Is that to characterize the feeling? (I didn't like my intervention, too much interpretation.)

Julie: I could use red (picking up the red crayon).

I wondered if it meant anger, but did not ask. I was pushing too hard and interfering with her thoughts and feelings. I decided to slow down. I just sat there at the table and let Julie take over. It was slow, but she did it. I had to bracket my impatience. It made me talk too much.

Julie: What do you want me to do?

Her dependency was in sharp contrast with the aggressive behavior she associated with being male. Too extreme. Females did not have to be dependent. I wanted her to know that. I had confronted her about her dependency numerous times.

I just looked at her and raised one eyebrow. She knew what I meant.

Slowly she started to draw a little row of stick figures stretching across the page (Figure 3). She did this very slowly and with a clenched fist. Her movements were jerky. When she reached the end of the page, the crayon broke. She seemed startled. I wanted her to go on.

Dr. Doyle: That's okay, Julie. You are doing well.

She picked up a yellow crayon and drew long hair on every other figure in the row. I was fascinated. They were gender drawings!

Figure 3
Julie's Gender Drawing

There were no genitals and they were not very sexual, but every other one was female. Julie put down the crayon, walked over to a beanbag, and sat down. I followed her with the picture in my hand. Sitting down in the bean bag opposite her, I spoke.

Dr. Doyle: Tell me about the picture. (I was careful not to lead her.)
Julie (looking at me with a dull, steady gaze and speaking slowly): They are inside my head. That's the way I am.

There were many possible interpretations of the drawing. I knew she wasn't bisexual or transsexual. I wasn't going to hazard a guess, it was too much like fishing. I waited.

Julie didn't say anything more during the session. She just rested in the beanbag. We did our little stretch, which had become a ritual, and broke for the day. I dated the picture and put it in her folder.

In the months that followed, there were many other drawings expressing Julie's ambivalence and anxiety about being a woman. Gradually, she began to understand that she had options other than her parental role models. She did not have to be the ineffectual, exploitable victim, nor the exploitive and abusive predator.

It became clear that Julie had strong, persistent sexual arousal feelings that she could not satisfy by masturbation alone. She attempted a lesbian solution, but it did not work for her. In fact, it seem to increase her anxiety and confusion. She felt contempt and disgust for any woman who would permit her to see or touch her breasts and/or genitals. Julie also experienced strong feelings of self-hatred and degradation if anyone, woman or man, saw or touched her sexual parts. Her anger at not being able to experience sexual gratification was mounting.

Julie: I can't listen to the people I work with talk about sex or close relationships anymore. Yesterday, I walked out of a session. . . .

This was an opening I could not resist. I had to address the underlying issue of Julie's career choice. At this point she was damaging her clients as well as herself.

Dr. Doyle (sighing deeply): Do you want to continue working as a counselor?

Julie: I applied for a job at a nursery last week. They called me this morning. I'll be unpacking and watering plants.

I was surprised and pleased that she had taken the initiative in this area of her life, but I didn't want to expend more session time talking about it.

Dr. Doyle: Good for you, Julie. Now you'll be able to focus more consistently on your sexual identity issue.

Julie: Well, there's something else I have to tell you. I started to drink Friday night. I went to a bar on Main Street. There was a guy there who bought me some drinks. He asked me if I wanted to make twenty . . . I did it. (She laughed, or rather cackled.) Twenty dollars. (She looked at me, waiting for my condemnation and disapproval.)

Dr. Doyle: I'm wondering if you felt genital excitement? Could you tell whether you orgasmed, or did the alcohol mask any good feelings you might have had?

Not very smooth, but it was a good response. No judgment. I had focused on her primary issue, what she wanted to feel sexually with a man.

Julie: I was too drunk.

Julie smiled, something she didn't do very often. She was obviously pleased with my acceptance of how she had chosen to work on her sexuality.

Internally, I was not entirely pleased. This was clearly not the beginning of a meaningful relationship for Julie. It was, however, a sexual experience with a man that Julie could talk about without anxiety, and she didn't seem totally disgusted with herself. In fact, she was proud that she had been sexual with a man.

Dr. Doyle: Could you handle having sex with a man without the alcohol? It would be another step toward normal sex.

I didn't add, "and eliminate playing the part of a prostitute," although it was on my mind. Maybe that type of degradation, that is, being paid for sex, would be healthier for Julie, than being totally exploited sexually as she had been in the past by her father and countless other men.

Julie: I've never done it without alcohol or drugs.

She lapsed into silence, her facial expression changed. The dull, dead look returned to her eyes. I could see her regressing.

"Let's draw," I said. I always put crayons and paper on the table for her sessions. We moved from the bean bags to the table. Julie picked up a blue crayon. This was different; she had used only black, red, and yellow before. I didn't comment. I had grown to respect Julie for the initiative and responsibility she was taking in therapy. Working very slowly, which was trying for an impatient therapist like myself, she colored the whole paper blue.

Julie: This is blue sky. I can see it.

Too vague, I thought, what does this have to do with sex?

Dr. Doyle: I don't see anything sexual in that picture.
Julie (smiling): I do.

She drew an angel-like figure with long yellow hair, obviously female, flying in the blue sky.

It still didn't look sexual to me until I realized the flying angel represented Julie, obviously a girl but not yet a woman. The picture had a mood of optimism, even though it seemed a little sugary sweet to me. It was much like the way Walt Disney would portray sex: fantasy-like with no details.

She didn't want to talk about it, so we did our stretching exercises, which I had expanded to include several more yoga stretches. I was not surprised to learn that Julie had enrolled in a coed yoga class at the community college. Her body image was improving. She still wore pants and shirts, but the cross-dressing had stopped. She chose brighter colors and was beginning to lose a little weight. She did not wear makeup, but had added small earrings.

Julie was accepting her femininity, but she wasn't being sexual. She had occasional fantasies about having enjoyable sex with men now, but no action in real life. Had she reached a plateau? I was beginning to think about termination of our sessions. Perhaps Julie needed a group instead of individual work to help her go on and relate sexually with men in a normal way.

Julie had joined an ACOA (Adult Children of Alcoholics) group. She also began to spend time with an older man who supervised her at the greenhouse where she worked. He was fifteen years her senior. I asked her if they had sexualized the relationship.

Julie: No. We slept together a couple of weekends ago when we were camping out, but we both had our clothes on. Nothing happened.

Dr. Doyle: What about touching? Is there much of that?

Julie: We've kissed a couple of times and hug a lot.

I was struck with the wholesome, adolescent nature of their relationship.

Dr. Doyle: Julie, it sounds like the kind of relationship you missed when you were growing up.

Julie (smiling and nodding yes): How old am I?

It was a significant question. Julie had been regressed, both sexually and socially. Because of that, normal development had not occurred. She had not gone through the stages and accomplished the tasks necessary to prepare her for adult sexuality. She seemed to sense this, even though she did not articulate it directly.

Dr. Doyle (humorously): Somewhere between seventeen and eighteen.

Julie: Old enough to have sex?

Dr. Doyle (nodding): Yes.

There was an awareness on both our parts that what had just occurred between us was a symbolic reenactment of an idealized parent-child relationship. She had asked her mother, whose opinion she respected, if it was okay to have intercourse. She had been given permission and could proceed like a good girl. She had always wanted to be a good girl, but she had been afraid to, because she didn't want to be like her mother. She wanted more respect and power, in sex and in life.

Our sessions were fewer now; we were meeting on a monthly basis. Julie reported having a sexual encounter with the man she had been seeing.

Julie: He really cares about me. You know, he wanted me to feel good. It's never been like that before. I can't believe how much I felt. And I was sober.

It was quite a different Julie that I now saw. She looked like a woman, and she was enjoying the sexual pleasures she deserved. But there had not been a miraculous recovery. She could relate only to an older man, who at this point did not pose a physical threat to her. She had accomplished a great deal in therapy. Her gender identity disorder no longer ruled her life, although the scars were there forever. Her psychosexual disorder had robbed her of choices she otherwise might have made regarding motherhood, career, and countless other options usually available to women.

9
William and Marie: Sibling Incest, Sexual Masochism, and Sexual Sadism (DSM-III-R-302.83; DSM-III-R-302.84)

William and Marie experienced abnormal sexual inclinations and behaviors. Brother and sister, they felt strong sexual arousal for each other but no one else. They had sexualized their relationship when they were children. William was seven years older than his sister, Marie, and had begun to initiate her into sex play when she was five. He knew he was doing something "wrong," but she had had no idea that she was misbehaving. She thought it was just a game, a secret game that they did in private and never talked about. It wasn't until she was nine that she realized she was "bad" for "playing nasty" with William. Marie enjoyed the feelings she had during their sex play but began to think of herself as "bad" because of the secrecy involved. Sex was bad, and she was bad.

William also felt guilty, doubly so because he had taught his little sister to "play nasty" with him. He had been initiated into sex play by a teenage babysitter when he was nine. The babysitter had fondled him and taught him how to masturbate himself. Unlike his sister Marie, at the outset he knew it was wrong, but he enjoyed the feelings and told no one. Later he repeated what he had learned and eroticized his sister's response, giving her the same inclination.

Incidents like these are common enough and do not always lead to psychosexual disorder. Usually children go on to have sexual experiences with appropriate partners and the guilt recedes into the past, along with the memories of the incidents themselves. This did not occur with William and Marie. What combination of circumstances prevented them from overcoming this early learning and going on to normal sexual expression?

I puzzled over this question many times during the years that I worked with them. We met for the first time in a joint session. The first thing I noticed was the similarity in their appearances: dark eyes and short, dark hair, his sprinkled with gray and hers slightly longer and uncurled. They were dressed in the same colors. He had on blue jeans and a black sweater; she wore black pants and a blue sweater. They were not touching. However, I could sense an unusual closeness, something about the way they looked at me and each other.

"I'm Doctor Doyle," I said. They said nothing. "Come into my office." I turned, and they followed me. After they were seated together on a couch facing me, I broke the tension that was building in the room.

Dr. Doyle: Tell me what is troubling you.

William (speaking first): We are related. I'm her brother.

I nodded to encourage him. She broke in.

Marie: We sleep together.

I should have been startled, but I wasn't. I was focused on the anxiety in their eyes and the tension in their bodies. They seemed to be holding their breath. I slouched a little in my chair and breathed deeply.

Dr. Doyle: Relax a little bit, it will be easier to talk.

I stretched my shoulders a little to model what I was suggesting. It worked. They moved, breathed, and started to tell me their story and what they wanted from counseling.

When I attended to the content, it did seem overwhelming. I bracketed my feeling, reminding myself that I didn't have to solve their problem, just lead them through the process, help them understand themselves, and order their feelings so they could decide what to do.

Their feelings were very complex. Their mother had been a young woman when she came to this country. She married an enlisted military man. She was timid, fearful, and prone to violent outbursts of temper when her husband was away, which was frequent. The children were often the objects of her frustration, loneliness, and anger.

William learned early to take care of himself and look after his sister. He was nurturing, gentle, and very loving with Marie. But he could also be punitive and controlling. He would spank her, turning her over on his knee. This did not happen often because she was usually "good." He never really hurt or bruised her, and she did not seem to resent it; in fact, she seemed to receive reassurance from it. He acted as a surrogate parent for her. She felt that without him there was no one who really cared.

Marie: He did it only to teach me a lesson and always hugged me afterward. (She started to say something else and then stopped. William looked uneasy.)

Dr. Doyle: Was there anything sexual about that for either one of you?

They looked at each other. A private communication of some kind seemed to be occurring. The silence built. I thought I could have asked that a little less directly. My first reaction when they were describing the spanking incidents was that the incidents were sexual and that they wanted to tell me something more, but were hesitating. My question was intended to facilitate their response. They just sat there looking at me. I remembered the injunction for beginning therapists: "Never ask a question that could be answered yes or no." It could cut off communication. But, I thought, it didn't really apply here. A clarification was needed in order to understand the problem and plan treatment. I was rationalizing.

I didn't know what to do, so I did nothing. William finally spoke.

William: That's our problem. Now every time we have sex she wants to be spanked or spank me.

Marie: Not every time. You like it that way too. Don't blame me for everything.

I didn't want to get distracted and drawn into discussing their relationship dynamics. I refocused on the point.

Dr. Doyle: Tell me about the spankings. How do you feel when you are being spanked?

Marie: Guilty. I feel bad but excited. He never really hurts me, but I want him to. Afterwards he rubs my bottom and we have sex.

I looked at William. He was silent for a while. The minutes seemed to stretch endlessly. I waited.

William: She hits me harder and uses a belt. I don't hit her as hard and I only use my hand. This is one of our problems. I think she really wants to hurt me.

He directed his glance toward his sister. Marie said nothing and remained motionless. I observed a very slight smile play about her lips. Should I comment on it and explore her feelings, or save that for a private session with her? William solved my dilemma.

William: She doesn't get excited unless I'm really hurting, and it seems to be getting worse. She made me bleed last time. Sometimes I think she wants to kill me. I'm afraid to let her tie me up anymore.

I knew he could go on and that it undoubtedly would be therapeutic for him to do so, but there were two clients in the room. I could feel Marie's anxiety building. I had to give her a chance to respond. I didn't want to further engage her defenses, so I softly said her name.

Dr. Doyle: Marie . . .

Marie: It's true. I'm really scared it is getting worse. For almost a year now, my fantasies have involved tying him up and beating him until he is almost dead. . . . I never used to. . . .

She was crying now, quietly, tears running down her face.

William, reaching for a tissue from the box on the floor, moved closer to her, handed it to her, and put his arm around her. She leaned against him, accepting his comforting.

Dr. Doyle (sighing): It's time for us to break. I'll see you separately next week.

William nodded. We scheduled our appointments. He laid my check on the couch beside him, and led Marie from the room.

Numerous issues had been raised in this session. Our culture does not allow sexual activity between persons with a blood relationship. My clients, however, did not seem at all concerned about the incestuous nature of their relationship. Most clients whose sexuality has been affected by incest consider it a problem. Neither William or Marie indicated they wanted to end their relationship, nor were they markedly disturbed by their incestuous behavior. They were, however, extremely distressed by Marie's sexual sadism.

As I was to learn in subsequent sessions, they both also suffered from sexual masochism. William's symptoms were more severe than his sister's in this category. However he showed no signs of sexual sadism.

The complexity of the case seemed overwhelming. Their psychological assessments revealed little other than slight antisocial tendencies. As is often the case with psychosexual disorders, there was no psychosis.

William did not believe that their sexual disorders were the result of anxiety over the incest taboo. At age 40, when he entered therapy with me, he was convinced that despite the cultural prohibition, his sexual relationship with his sister was okay—even healthy.

I had to be on guard not to engage in intellectual arguments or discussion about the Egyptian Ptolemaic period, or any other point he was using to rationalize his behavior. Instead, I focused on his masochism, his fears that Marie would kill him or that he would severely injure himself. He preferred acting out his sexual fantasies with her, but he would also sometimes masturbate, thinking about previous times when she had tied up, blindfolded, and beaten him. At times his masturbatory behavior included looping a cord around his neck.

William: The humiliation gives me powerful arousal feelings. The feelings are so intense that everything else fades away. All I want is that feeling.

Dr. Doyle: You seem to regret having it (reflecting his feeling and planting a suggestion).

William: Afterwards (nodding in affirmation). I'd like to go back to the way it used to be, when we could just spank a little and then have fun.

Dr. Doyle: The way you said that, William, . . . sounded as if you felt guilt about even having sex with Marie, and that you had to be punished in order to go on and enjoy it.

William (looking at me and shaking his head no): It's humiliation, not guilt, that arouses me.

I knew better than to argue with him, but I kept planting seeds of doubt throughout the therapy to make him question the incestuous relationship itself, not just the masochism and sadism it had evoked within him and his sister.

Usually we met together, although there were some individual sessions that focused on their specific disturbances. In one such session with Marie, she expressed unusually strong resentment toward William and actually focused on the incestuous bond.

Marie: I was just a child when it started, only five. He ruined my life.

I was surprised. It was the opening I had hoped for, but I was afraid I would blow it. If I said anything, she would become defensive again, protective of herself, of William, and of the relationship. I said nothing, just looked at her and sat very still.

She went on:

Marie: Sometimes I wonder what it would be like to have a normal life. Not marriage or children, God forbid, but something besides work and him.

That word, "him," came out very forcefully, almost like a hiss. Her eyes narrowed, her jaw clenched. She started to breathe deeply, looking as if she hated me. I knew she was seeing William, not me, and I wanted to use this moment to therapeutic advantage. She had regressed to the past. I didn't want to force her back to the present and lose the opportunity to bring about some healing, so I layered in a different response, the nurturing that she had never received from her mother.

Dr. Doyle: You didn't choose this for yourself. As a child, you didn't understand. Don't blame yourself for what happened then.

It was as if I had presented her with a gift. Her face softened. She sat there looking at me. The feeling in the room was very strong, and yet I felt relief.

Marie: I didn't do anything wrong, did I?

An alarm went off in my mind. Choicepoint. I wasn't sure what content she was focusing on. I couldn't affirm her sadistic feeling and behaviors, nor did I want to affirm the incestuous relationship. I said nothing, and she answered her own question.

Marie: Well, not then as a child, but now as an adult. I'm thirty-three, and I've never had sex with anyone but my brother, and I'm turning into a monster.

She was confused. There were several thoughts and feelings conflicting within her. Aware of the loss of normal relationships the incestuous bond had cost her, she was beset with a rush of feelings. The danger of helping her clarify was that I would interrupt the flow of feelings. I waited. She was making odd sounds now; like heavy swallowing or gulping. Not really crying. Finally she lay down on the couch and turned her back to me. I sighed; she needed to rest and so did I.

There was a change in her after that session. Although she continued to live with William and sleep with him in the house their parents had left them, she no longer had sex with him.

This was a problem for William. He was very angry with me, insisting that I had turned her against him and judged their relationship as bad. I feared that they would drop out of therapy before their gains were consolidated, and that he would convince her to resexualize their relationship. But they continued to come week after week, sitting farther and farther apart on the couch as if to symbolize the rift between them.

William was not willing to come in for individual sessions anymore.

William: I won't stop her, but you're not going to get me in here alone.

He said he was afraid of my judgment, although I had said nothing to imply that he alone was responsible for the incest and the other sexual disorders that he and his sister had developed.

No matter how I tried to communicate acceptance, without which he could not change, he would not have it. Then he became depressed and talked about wanting to die and about how much better off Marie would be if he weren't around anymore.

Dr. Doyle: William, you've got a right to a life too. (Was I being drawn into his defensive manipulation or giving therapeutic reassurance? Thin line.)

Marie: I'm not mad at you. You probably never would have touched me if you hadn't been raped yourself. (We were both doing it, trying to appease him and make him feel better.)

William: None of that matters. The only thing I care about is that you won't have sex with me anymore. Everything has changed. I don't have anything to live for.

William's position was still that the incest was okay, even good, and that their only problem was Marie's sexual sadism. My interference through therapy had ruined everything. It was time for a confrontation.

Dr. Doyle: William, talk about what the loss of sex with Marie means to you. You act as if it were your whole life.

He was silent, looked at Marie, then down at his feet. Still nothing. I sighed, audibly, expressing my impatience.

William: It's what I've had instead of a life.

I was amazed, it had happened. He had dropped his denial. He had acknowledged that the incestuous relationship was a substitute for life.

Our next meeting was scheduled for them both, but William came alone. He was ready to explore his own feelings in depth, at last. He wanted to talk about his mother, so I listened. It was as if we were starting all over again. He recalled his mother's tantrums, how violent she had been. This time, however, when he described it, he showed more feelings. His voice trembled as he described how after a tantrum she would cry and lie down on the floor. She would motion to him to lie beside her, and they would make up that way. He remembered nothing overtly sexual, except for the intense relief he had felt that the tantrum was over.

William: We didn't touch each other or anything, but there was something weird, like we shouldn't have been doing that . . . like I felt with the babysitter.

Dr. Doyle: Not like what should happen between mother and child.

William: Yeah. She wasn't like other mothers. I felt like she was just there, but not a mother.

He pulled out his wallet and showed me a picture. At first I thought it was Marie, but it was his mother. A youngish, serious-looking woman with dark hair and eyes. Why was he still carrying it, I wondered.

Intuitively I knew he was telling me that Mother and Marie were blended in his mind and emotions. I wanted to ask him about it, but needed to avoid being too suggestive.

Dr. Doyle: I'm struck with the family resemblance.

William (nodding affirmatively): Often, during sex, it feels like Marie is Mother.

He looked at me and I nodded slightly, as if I already knew that. We sat silently.

William: I'm a mother fucker!

There was a lot of venom and anger in his voice.

Internally I was startled. William had never cursed in session before. Moreover, I always have trouble with such expressions. I thought about it. Maybe this was his way of crying, because there were no tears. I worried about that. I knew he had to feel deeply if healing were to occur. I took a chance.

Dr. Doyle: What does that mean?

William: It means I'm shit. I've dishonored my mother and fucked my sister. How can you sit in the same room with me?

Dr. Doyle: I feel a lot of respect for what you are doing right now.

William: What am I doing?

Dr. Doyle: Trying to cleanse yourself, make yourself whole.

He was grateful for the reassurance.

Things moved quickly after that. Marie found an apartment and moved out of the house. William continued to live there for almost a year before he put the house up for sale. They continued in counseling, mostly individual sessions, trying to establish separate identities. It was very difficult for both of them. They experienced a great deal of grieving and self-doubt. They were both very naive socially. Neither William nor Marie had experienced the normal socialization process. No friends, no dating, and only a slight awareness of what life could be outside of the restrictive environment within which they had lived.

Poorly defined sexual boundaries between family members had made it likely that their childish sex play, which in itself had been within normal limits, would combine with other elements in their learning and develop into psychosexual disorder.

Marie's sadism continued to be a problem. She needed a lot of encouragement to date. Her arousal response continued to be linked to fantasies of inflicting psychological and physical suffering upon her sexual partners. Most of the males she was attracted to looked like William, or had his coloring.

Marie: Am I ever going to get over this? I've tried dating blond men. I've done everything you've recommended . . . masturbating and fantasizing myself in a loving sexual encounter. It just isn't exciting.

I didn't have an answer. Marie wanted a normal sex life, but nothing in her early learning had prepared her for that. All we could do was try to fill in the developmental gaps with healthier attitudes and experiences, which would gradually move her toward sexual expression.

The prognosis for Marie was definitely guarded. Sexual sadism is chronic and can recur again and again in a person's life. We had interrupted the course of the disorder and made some significant environmental changes. Sex education and social experience had altered her attitudes and behavior. But the intense sexual urges and sexually arousing fantasies of inflicting pain on others were still dangerous, and severely limited the life experiences she could enjoy. She felt that marriage and children were not options for her. She was proud of herself for breaking away from William and trying to make a new life for herself.

William was more cautious. He felt his best solution was to avoid all sexual contact. Sexual masochism is also chronic. William continued to have fantasies of being humiliated and made to suffer. He now tried to distract himself from these thoughts and rarely allowed himself to masturbate, for fear the urges would recur and overwhelm him.

I felt sadness for both of them. Although they had made a great deal of progress in overcoming their psychosexual disorder, the impact of childhood learning had left an indelible effect on their lives.

My work with them was over. It had been successful, and yet I was not satisfied. They deserve more than I was able to give them. Can the effects of the childhood patterns of sexual maladjustment ever be completely erased?

10

Roy: Homosexual Pedophilia (DSM-III-R-302.20)

Roy was in crisis the first time I saw him. He was frightened and desperate, his defenses were down, so he spoke openly, perhaps for the first time in his life.

He was a homosexual who had all the features of a pedophiliac. He had involved himself with prepubescent males, who had little awareness of the long-term effect this sex play would have on their development.

Roy preferred eight- or nine-year-olds and seemed to lose interest in the boys he victimized when they developed a full crop of pubic hair. His arousal feelings diminished when he no longer felt the same degree of power over his victims. He had extremely intense sexual urges and continual fantasies about young boys.

His usual approach was to become a "friend of the family" and develop a trusting relationship, which he later betrayed by seducing and coercing the young males into sex play. This involved touching their genitals and persuading them to suck his penis.

He would swear them to secrecy, saying they would both be in trouble if anyone knew. He had repeated this behavior for many years without being caught, although some of the boys' families had eventually limited his contact with their sons, giving various reasons. He had never before been charged with sexual abuse. This is not unusual. Parents frequently choose to protect themselves and their children from the unpleasantness that ensues from an investigation done by the authorities. Although their silence leads to guilt feelings, most parents avoid reporting sex crimes against their children.

This time, however, Roy was arrested. He had molested a young boy on the soccer team he coached. As in the past, Roy had used his position as a junior high school physical education teacher to gratify his sexual needs. This time the father of the boy learned what had happened, after his son had refused to attend physical education class or participate in team activities, even though he loved the game. The police were called and Roy was arrested.

After being charged and released on bail, he came to my office for consultation. He had called first to tell me about his predicament. I think he wanted to give me a chance to refuse to see him. He needed to assure himself that I would listen.

Roy: They won't let me teach anymore, will they?

Dr. Doyle: I don't know.

Roy: Can you help me?

I looked at him and realized that I wouldn't be able to help him if I saw him only as a pedophiliac. I have many negative associations with perpetrators of sexual crimes against children, but I had to understand him as a person in order to help him. I had to make contact with his humanity to be effective.

Dr. Doyle: Tell me about yourself.

Roy: What do you want to know?

Dr. Doyle: What brought you to this point in your life?

I didn't like the question, too vague, but it was a way to get started. He relaxed a bit. I had given him a choice about where to start.

Roy: Well, it happened to me. I was molested by a priest.

Dr. Doyle: He taught you how to do it (and thought to myself, like a link in a chain).

Roy: Yes. (Surprised and relieved that I understood.) I don't mean that I was destined to do it, but I did learn about sex that way, and it didn't really hurt me.

I had trouble with that. He had been hurt even if he wouldn't admit it. Arrest, imprisonment, and loss of freedom were fearful things. I was arguing with him in my mind. That would get me nowhere.

Dr. Doyle: You seem to be hurting now.

He looked at me. The rationalizations ceased. He held his head in his hands.

Dr. Doyle: You'll feel better after you tell me about the sexual molestation that led to your arrest.

He looked up at me and started to describe how he had taken the boy, Mark, one of his students, home from practice. It was several hours before Mark's parents would be home from work. As they had done many times before, they showered and lounged around Mark's room in their underwear, talking about the game. Mark was lying on the bed, and Roy was seated near the end of the bed. Roy started to rub Mark's feet and legs, slowly approaching his genital area. The boy just lay there and let Roy remove his briefs and start to massage his penis. Roy put his face very close to the boy's crotch, so he could see the changes as the boy's small penis became hard. Taking the penis into his mouth, he sucked until Mark had an ejaculation.

He had done the same thing many times to other boys. They never talked about it, and Roy always concluded that the boys enjoyed it. This time, he asked Mark to "do" him. Mark tried, but when Roy ejaculated, he gagged and ran to the bathroom. He was there only a few minutes, and when he came out, he was composed. Roy left soon afterwards. Three days later, police officers came to Roy's house and arrested him.

There wasn't much feeling in Roy's voice as he spoke, but his face paled and his hands started to tremble.

Roy: What am I going to do? (His voice had a thin, childlike quality.)

Dr. Doyle: We're going to talk about it until we understand more about your sexuality. That process will help release your feelings. Then it will be clearer.

My voice was firm. I had made a connection with him. I saw him as a person in anguish. I didn't know how long it would last, but I was no longer judging him. This enabled me to lead him through the tortured process of exploring his sexual development, so that he could better understand himself.

There were many times during our weekly sessions that I lost my way and felt judgmental. For the most part, I bracketed my feelings successfully, and he never knew what I was experiencing. But on one such occasion he confronted me. He had been talking about how much his job had meant to him, and how much he longed to go back to it.

I had said nothing, nor had I looked at him in any special way. But he sensed my reaction.

Roy: You don't think I should teach again, do you?

Dr. Doyle: No, I don't. It's not safe for you or the children you would work with.

Roy: You tell it the way it is, don't you!

I nodded yes and sighed. We both felt sad. This was the way it was between us. We never pretended that he wasn't at risk for committing the same crime again.

Roy had no sexual arousal response to women or even adult males, who could be consenting partners. Was Roy homosexual, or did he simply feel inadequate about his ability to act as an adult male sexually?

Behavior modification would have to begin at once. Part of our treatment approach involved homework assignments where Roy would masturbate while looking at erotic pictures of age-appropriate partners. Pictures of both adult males and adult females were utilized, in order to eroticize him to more acceptable sex partners.

Concurrently, we worked to extinguish his arousal response to young males. A nurse clinician on my staff gave him an emetic solution to induce vomiting. Simultaneously, she presented him with pictures of prepubescent male genitals. The solution did cause him to vomit, and he reported less interest in sexualizing with young males.

Although he began to feel more sexual interest in women, and could fantasize having powerful feelings during sexual encounters with them, he was unable to approach an adult woman in a social situation. If he felt she would have romantic or sexual expectations of him, he felt fear, which prevented his sexual response from developing. As part of his treatment, Roy attended social gatherings for singles on a regular basis. However, even though he developed friendships with women he dated, there was insufficient time to clarify whether a romantic or sexual bond could develop. According to Roy's report, erotic fantasies of young boys ceased. As far as I could tell, Roy was becoming asexual.

Roy was very cooperative and did everything he was asked to do. He didn't want to go to jail, and hoped that his cooperation in treatment would increase the possibility that the charge against him would be dropped or that he would get a light sentence, quickly followed by probation.

Roy's family and friends were supportive during the whole process. They started a fund to help pay for his legal and counseling fees. Many expressed a willingness to come to counseling or do anything that would help him. We did have family sessions, and I did meet with some of his friends. Everyone thought that he was a nice guy, always ready to help — the kind of person who would never hurt anyone.

It was all true. He was a nice guy; with the exception of his psychosexual disorder, he had never hurt anyone. Unfortunately, every time Roy had sexually molested a young male, there was a strong possibility that his victim would also become a perpetrator of sexual crimes against children. The chain would go on and on.

When we talked about this aspect of his behavior, Roy seemed undisturbed, as if the only problem was in getting caught. To him the problem was not the behavior itself, but the way society saw it.

Roy: It feels good to them. I know it does. I would never hurt them.

Dr. Doyle: I think you were hurt by that priest who molested you. (I knew I had to avoid talking about "them.")

Roy: What do you mean?

Dr. Doyle: What do you think your life would have been like if you had learned about sex in a normal way?

His expression changed. My focused concern for him in my intervention had touched him. He dropped his denial.

Roy: I've thought about that. I might have been okay. I'm a good person and a good teacher.

He started to cry, not very loudly, but with many tears. His nose started to run. I didn't move. Speaking, touching him, or giving him a tissue would have interrupted the process. I was aware of how much older than his thirty-eight years he looked, and how limited his life had been. I felt his pain.

Our session time was running out, I had to bring him out of his feelings and prepare him to leave. We had about eight minutes.

Dr. Doyle: Tell me about the tears, Roy.

Roy (looking up at me): I'm crying for myself. Not them.

Dr. Doyle (nodding yes): I know.

He had finally admitted that being sexually abused as a boy had damaged him.

After that we moved our sessions to the playroom. I had suggested this to him earlier, but he had resisted. I wanted to help him remember parts of his early childhood, so that he could reacquaint himself with the boy he had been. My objective was to reawaken his innocence and layer in a stronger sense of right and wrong. Something had gone awry in his early development, and he had never formed an adequate conscience. Moreover, he was still suffering from cognitive dissonance. A priest had sexually molested him. Priests were good. How could sexual molestation of young boys be bad if priests did it? It all ran together in his mind. He was still a confused child. That's why the playroom would be effective. He scoffed at the idea but went along with it, mainly to humor me.

I had designed the playroom for regression work, both with children and adults. It was simply furnished, with two large beanbags, in which Roy and I usually sat as we talked. There was a round table cut down to child size, with matching chairs. A toy shelf with a small selection of toys stood in one corner. A nursery clock, shaped like Noah's ark, was on the wall. There was very little else in the room.

The first time Roy saw the room, he seemed astonished. I closed the door behind us and sat down in one of the chairs. I remained silent, letting him react without interference. He was quiet a long time, walked around the room, looked at the toys, and selected a small wooden pull toy, an animal of some sort.

Roy: I used to have something like this.

(I smiled slightly, remaining silent.)

Roy: What am I supposed to do?

Dr. Doyle: Nothing special. Just let yourself feel your reaction to being here.

Roy: It's like being in first grade again. (He lay down on the floor and started to laugh.) I can see it all now. Judge, don't send me to jail. I'm cured. I went back to first grade and learned how to be a good boy.

He laughed harder, or at least I thought he was laughing until he began to gasp for air. Then it sounded more like crying, but he began to cough and brought himself out of it.

Roy: Doyle, what now?

Dr. Doyle: Let's draw pictures.

I got some primary crayons and paper from the shelf and sat down at the table. He came over, seated himself, and looked at me for direction, much as a child would do.

Dr. Doyle: Draw a picture of yourself. I'll watch.

He drew a mean face with the tongue sticking out (Figure 4).

Dr. Doyle: You look mad.
Roy: I'm not mad.

He got up from the table, picked up a softball, and threw it at me. I caught it and threw it back. We threw the ball back and forth; each time he threw it harder. Finally he threw it at me. I barely caught it and laid it down.

Dr. Doyle: We can't play anymore if you are that rough.

He laughed. I was struck with how regressed he looked, about seven or eight, like a boy.

Figure 4
Roy's Mean Face

Dr. Doyle: Roy, tell me what you're feeling?

Roy: Nothing, just having fun.

Dr. Doyle: Did you play like that when you were little?

Roy: Sometimes, with my sister. I would scare her. She wore her hair in a pony tail, sort of like you.

I was internally startled. I knew the transference was at work, because I wore my hair in a braid pulled to one side. I said nothing. He curled up in one of the beanbags and started to talk about his sister.

Roy: She was born with some kind of disease, something wrong with her spine. She was in a wheelchair before she died. We were poor, but the parish priests helped us a lot. They brought us food, got her medical care, came to our house a lot. That's how I met Father Patrick. He was very kind to us. . . . (His voice trailed off. He stared at the clock on the wall. His face crumpled a bit.) That's the ark, isn't it?

Dr. Doyle: You were thinking about Father Patrick, but I think you got scared.

Silence. Our time was almost up, but I didn't want to break. My lunch hour followed. I decided to continue working past our allotted time, something I did not allow my training associates to do. I was hungry, and as my stomach started to growl, I became preoccupied with myself and lost contact with Roy's internal frame of reference. He was feeling scared and confused about Father Patrick, and I was feeling hungry. I tried to force myself back on track.

Dr. Doyle: Tell me about Father Patrick.

As soon as I said it, I knew it was over. I should have focused on his feeling about being scared, or kept my mouth shut and let him go on by himself.

Roy: I forgot what I was saying.

He got up from the beanbag and put the toy back on the shelf. He was thirty-eight years old again; the eight-year-old was gone. But I was to see and work with the eight-year-old many times in the months that followed. Although we played with clay and puppets, reenacting portions of Roy's boyhood recollections, the adult male in him was also present. In most of our sessions we addressed both the adult and the child within. We summarized and speculated about the impact of the sexual molestation on Roy's development.

Roy: I used to have this dream, where Father Patrick was God, and could not do wrong.

Dr. Doyle: Talk about the dream. What can you remember?

Roy: Oh, I still have it sometimes. I . . . (He looked at me and hesitated. I waited, and he started to fidget. I wondered if he was having wet dreams.)

Dr. Doyle: There's something you don't want to tell me. (I smiled a bit, letting him know it was okay.)

Roy: I feel like I'm talking to my mother. . . . Anyway, I always wake up from the dream with a hard-on.

Dr. Doyle: It's a sexual dream?

Roy: Yeah. He's masturbating me, like he did the first time.

Dr. Doyle: This is where you get confused?

I had adopted the method of stating my suggestions in the form of a question so he could agree or disagree as I led him along. I didn't want to engage his defenses.

We had reached a point where I could layer in a new interpretation of what had happened and clear up the confusion he had lived with all these years. How should I start? Roy gave me my opening.

Roy: I used to believe in God. Sometimes I still do.

He fell silent. His face crumpled; the tears came. His nose started to run. He wiped it on his sleeve, like a little boy.

I leaned forward slightly and touched his hand.

Dr. Doyle: It's hard to believe in God when his representative does something wrong. (He looked at me, ready to follow.) Father Patrick did do something wrong, even though he may have been a good and kind man in many ways. He was very wrong to touch you sexually. God did not approve. You know that, don't you?

I wondered if I had said too much. Maybe that last line was overkill; I sounded more like a mother than a therapist. Roy was holding my hand now. When I had touched him, he had moved his other hand toward mine without reciprocating my touch. When I said, "God would not approve," he clasped my hand and held on to it. I was ready to quit, but I had to bring him out of it. We sat there quietly for a while. Roy spoke first.

Roy: This was a good session.
Dr. Doyle: Yes, you worked hard.

In our next session Roy started to play with the soft puppets. I asked him to reenact the time when Father Patrick first molested him. He laughed nervously, as he usually did when he was scared. He laid one puppet down on the floor face up and slammed the other one, which I assumed was Father Patrick, face down on top. Then, he looked at me defiantly.

Dr. Doyle: Is that how it happened; did he hurt you?
Roy: No. It felt good. He licked me all over like a dog, then he sucked me until I came. I'll never forget the way it felt the first time. Like an explosion, a wonderful explosion.
Dr. Doyle: I wonder if you were scared. You were so young.
Roy (nodding yes): But it felt good; that's what I remember the most.

I wanted to erode the positive aspects of that memory, but I had to go very slowly.

Dr. Doyle: Even though it felt good, I wish that hadn't happened to you. You were too young to make a choice for yourself.

He was quiet. Our work was far from complete. Roy was just beginning to differentiate himself from Father Patrick, whose identity had blended with that of God. The intense eroticism Roy had felt when he was first introduced to sex by Father Patrick had blurred the distinction in his childish mind. Thereafter, if sex and Father Patrick were bad, God was also bad. Conversely, if God were good, sex and Father Patrick were also good.

Since Roy had received very little positive sex education to balance his early learning, the overgeneralization had remained intact and significantly altered his sexual development. Had this not occurred, it is altogether possible that Roy would have experienced normal heterosexual development.

Our regression work in the playroom was aimed at enabling Roy to discriminate between the associations he had with sex, Father Patrick, and God. Moreover, we had to clearly establish that children are not appropriate sex objects for adults. During our sessions in the playroom, I taught Roy what he had not learned as a child — that his body and his genitals were his own and no one had a right to touch them, and that if any adult, even a relative, teacher, or priest, attempted to do so, it was wrong and should be reported to parents and/or police immediately.

This was a little too simplistic for Roy.

Roy: I didn't know it was against the law, but that probably wouldn't have meant much to me.

I wasn't going to argue with him, so I just reflected content.

Dr. Doyle: No clear distinction between right and wrong?

Roy: My parents were good people. They taught me a lot about right and wrong, and a lot about God. They never talked about sex, . . . but I'm not going to blame them. It doesn't matter anyway. My trial is next month. My attorney can't get me another continuance. I've been lucky to have my freedom for so long.

He sat there quietly in the beanbag, holding a soft puppet, as he often did. He was feeling fearful and hopeless, as if he knew his trial would have an unfavorable outcome.

Where was his anger? As with many of my other clients with psychosexual disorders, this shouldn't have happened to him. Roy deserved another chance, but he couldn't have another chance without endangering others. Even now, with all the work we had done, I couldn't be sure that he wouldn't sexually molest another child. Habit is strong, and our therapeutic intervention had been of relatively short duration compared to the many years that Roy had practiced pedophilia.

I felt a great deal of compassion for him, and I had to be careful not to feed my own anger into Roy. And I was angry, angry that I didn't have more time to work with him. I knew he would not receive adequate therapy in prison.

Roy: Will you be there (at the trial)? There's enough money in my fund to pay for your time.

He seemed to be pleading with me. I had mixed feelings. I had utilized the transference in therapy. There had been many times when he had seen me as a surrogate mother, someone who had taught him a clearer distinction between right and wrong. This had enabled him to rebuild some of the trust in authority that had been damaged when Father Patrick molested him. There had been an element of mysticism in the therapeutic process. He knew he was an adult, although he sometimes had the feelings of a child. He knew I was his therapist and not his mother, but the symbolism that had been evoked in the playroom had created a useful bond to reshape his early learning about sexuality. I knew what he was feeling. He wanted his mother to be there; he was scared. What could be more natural than a mother going to her son's trial? But I wasn't his mother. I was his therapist, and his own mother would be there.

Dr. Doyle: I'm not sure it would be the best thing.

Roy: I know you can't speak for me. My attorney says it would be best just to say I've been in therapy consistently with an expert on sexuality, rather than question you directly.

Dr. Doyle: How do you feel about that?

Roy: Okay. I know you wouldn't perjure yourself for me or anyone else. I really don't think I'd do it again. I just don't want to put anyone else through what's happened to me. Do you believe me?

I nodded yes and touched his hand, but in my mind I wasn't sure. He laid his head down on our clasped hands, a gesture he had developed during our work in the playroom. We sat quietly for a while. He did not press me for an answer about my presence at his trial.

Roy: It's going to seem strange not coming here anymore. So much has happened in this room. (He was talking about termination of counseling.)

Dr. Doyle (wanting to consolidate the changes he had made): What has happened in this room?

Roy (laughing): I found out I was a little boy. A confused little boy that had been mistreated and sodomized.

He was laughing, teasing me, like a bad little boy waiting to be corrected by his mother, or a middle-aged man saying goodbye to his therapist. He laughed again. I looked at him. I had hoped for more. I looked at him and sighed deeply, expressing impatience. He continued.

Roy: I know I was wrong. I should not have sexualized with those young boys. They were just as innocent as me. But I don't hate myself and I don't hate Father Patrick. Someone else probably screwed him up.

I did go to Roy's trial, although I didn't testify. He knew I was there, and it made him feel better. He was convicted, and he did go to jail.

Why did I go to his trial? The day it was scheduled I was overbooked, and it was hard for me to get away from the office; moreover, I don't like the downtown traffic. But I just couldn't let him

Figure 5
Playroom Door

down. Was it counter transference? Had my feelings become too involved? Ironically, as I had come to know Roy the pedophiliac as Roy the person, I had grown to like and respect him for the courage he had shown in therapy and the changes he had made.

A word about treatment. I believe that the gains Roy made were the result of regression therapy and of our relationship. I would not, however, have omitted the behavioral conditioning sessions aimed at reshaping his arousal response. His treatment was interrupted by his trial and imprisonment. I estimate that at least twice the time we had was needed to consolidate the therapeutic process.

Figure 6
Playroom

Figure 7
Regression Chest

PLAYROOM

All furnishings are symbolic. A simple design, sparse furnishings: a child-sized table and chairs, two beanbags, a corner shelf with generic toys, and a small regression chest in one corner. A nursery clock shaped like Noah's ark is on the wall.

On the outside of the door leading into the playroom, a stuffed owl is fastened, and there are two pegged coat racks, one at adult height and one at child height. (See Figure 5.) When leading a client to the playroom, the therapist remains silent, opens the door, slips in, and allows the client to react. (See Figure 6.)

Contents of the regression chest (Figure 7) are unique to each client. Items are selected to evoke client memories. Start with general memorabilia and proceed to more and more specific items relating to the traumatic incident that disrupted development.

Part 2
Theory and Method

11
Blueprint for Therapy

Envision yourself trying to plan treatment for a sexually disturbed client. Even though you have been trained to set aside or bracket your personal feelings and biases about sexual deviations from the norm, your thought processes are impaired. A judgmental attitude starts to build within you. You want to help this person, but you are having difficulty listening. You are aware that he or she has committed a sexual crime or engaged in a sexual act that you consider unacceptable. Your training prevents you from displaying an obvious negative reaction, but that takes energy on your part. Consequently, your understanding of the sexually disturbed client is imprecise. You might make erroneous assumptions, based on a faulty perception of your client's condition. To prevent this, you reframe your perception of this client as a victim of developmental misfortune.

Disruptions in sexual development must be identified, and addressed directly, if normal development is to resume. Utilizing a developmental blueprint to plan client-specific treatment also provides the therapist with knowledge and understanding that enhances empathic response, and helps to alleviate negative attitudes about and biases against the sexually disturbed.

My own experience with this type of reaction prompted me to establish a series of guidelines for applying developmental theory to the process of therapy. This method of perceiving my client's growth keeps me mindful of his or her humanity and mitigates the natural repulsion to deviation. Other essential components of successful treatment include (1) techniques for preventing enmeshment of client and therapist defense systems; (2) the use of appropriate and sexually explicit language; and (3) the management of sexual attraction between client and therapist.

Childhood sexual instincts are powerful. If left to develop without disturbance in a moderately benign and accepting environment, these sexual feelings will cause neither embarrassment, shame, nor harm to anyone. However, when normal development is interrupted by trauma, such as sexual abuse or exposure to violent or highly emotional sexual events, deviance from normal sexual development occurs. Without therapeutic intervention, the outcome predicted from that phase of development, and all subsequent phases, will be adversely affected. These disturbances rarely correct themselves. An unusually high state of psychological arousal occurs in situations of sexual trauma, such as sexual abuse. The high psychological arousal is due to the combination of the anxiety of helplessness felt by the victim and the erotic genital response. The intensity of these paired emotions can tax the coping powers of an adult, and is overwhelming to a child.

Actually, totally undisturbed sexual development rarely occurs. Negative sexual messages are the norm. Most children are subjected to such cultural messages as: Don't acknowledge sexual pleasure; don't talk about sex; don't use specific terms for private parts; don't acknowledge sexual acts such as intercourse and masturbation. Fortunately, if the messages are not accompanied by anger or excessive anxiety, their impact is not intense or lasting. Most children can incorporate parental and family injunctions about sexuality without significant disturbance of their sexual development. It is the norm to cloak sexuality with mystery and prohibition.

Deviance from normal sexual development is readily identified by a well-trained therapist with a working knowledge of developmental psychology. If students understand the practical value of theory, they are motivated to explore developmental psychology and apply it as a blueprint for therapeutic intervention. Many training associates with advanced degrees have commented on how much more interesting and exciting it would have been for them if, at the undergraduate level, they had understood the power that knowledge of sequential stages of development would give them to free people from pain and anguish.

Knowledge of the theory of sexual, social, cognitive, or moral development enables the therapist to identify the point at which a disturbance occurred and formulate an intervention that the client can absorb and integrate. For example, if a child were sexually abused between the ages two and seven, Jean Piaget's theory of cognitive development guides the therapist to understand the thought processes the child would have been capable of at the time the abuse occurred. At this age, the child functions in the preoperational stage and is limited to transductive reasoning, which is a rudimentary sorting process that involves making inferences or associations on the basis of a single attribute. Utilizing Piaget's explication of the child's level of thinking at the time the sexual molestation disturbed normal development, the therapist is equipped to approach the child within the client. It is then possible to direct therapeutic intervention to the exact point where relearning needs to occur. Moreover, the intervention is delivered in language and symbolism at the preoperational level, thus making it more likely that the child within the client will be reached. Trying to heal psychological wounds that occurred in childhood by talking to the client only in an adult manner does not address the developmental issue on its own terms. Polysyllabic words are lost on youngsters. There is little doubt that much therapy is ineffective for just this reason. The language prohibits understanding; communication is blocked; and therapy does not occur.

When we were children, our sexual feelings and instincts were capable of being awakened. Genital arousal occurred and was enjoyed by most of us when we were very young. These feelings are quite normal. Even if we do not follow the Freudian map that eroticizes different parts of our bodies at different stages of development, we generally accept the notion that failure to resolve a psychosexual conflict at any stage of development creates a fixation, or gap in learning, at that stage. Since psychosexual development occurs in sequential stages, we can pinpoint on the clinical map the point where development was arrested. Therapeutic intervention is planned to fill the gap caused by the disturbance, thus making it possible for normal development to resume.

Utilizing a map or chart based on predictable psychological

stages is a relatively simple process that even undergraduate students can accomplish as they gather information about specific events in a client's early life.

Early sexual feelings that children experience generally occur either through accidental discovery of self-stimulation or in association with parents, siblings, or extended family members. This can occur while being held, bathed, or nursed, with or without intent on the part of the caregiver. However, when those sexual sensations are charged with emotions such as anger, fear, or anxiety, a developmental crisis can occur that interferes with normal development in subsequent stages. For example, by using Erik Erikson's stages of psychosocial development as a guideline, the therapist can evaluate a client who has experienced sexual trauma in any of the first three stages of development. The evaluation consists of clarification of the hallmark feelings for each stage and their manifestations in the adult client. Based on behaviors observed in the adult, the therapist can ascertain how much imbalance has resulted and in approximately what stage the disruption occurred. Curative interventions can then be planned to "layer in" the foundation for more balanced behavior.

Using Eriksonian guidelines for the first six years of life, the therapist can search for specific qualities in the adult client, such as trust, autonomy, and initiative, or their counterpoints, mistrust, shame, and guilt. The oral sensory stage, from birth to twelve months, carries with it the task of balancing trust versus mistrust. In the muscular anal stage, ages twelve through thirty-six months, the developmental task is to balance autonomy versus shame. The locomotor genital stage, ages three to six years, must equalize initiative versus guilt.

When sexual trauma occurs in these early stages, significant disruption in development results. In Stage One, trust in self and others can be jeopardized and the constancy of sexual identity can be compromised. In Stage Two, traumatization by a homosexual pedophiliac, or even negative parental reaction to male or female genitals, can result in gender dysphoria or homosexual tendencies, where shame predominates autonomy. In Stage Three, locomotor genital, sexual traumatization interrupts and may prevent the development of initiative, and guilt will characterize the life of the adult.

Unfortunately sexual trauma may occur in two or more developmental stages in the same individual. The resulting damage to sexual identity formation is exponentially confounded. Although in these cases treatment strategies are necessarily more complex, the developmental maps are still the basic guidelines for identifying gaps and imbalances, as well as for targeting behaviors or new learning that must be "layered in" to replace the original faulty learning.

In applying developmental theory to plan treatment with Frank, the ego dystonic homosexual in Chapter 7, we see that he has considerably more mistrust than trust in both self and others. We also note his strong feelings of shame and guilt regarding his sexual attraction for males. Confirming this, we note that there is little evidence of the balancing side of the conflicts; trust, autonomy, and initiative are not present. We conclude that there are developmental gaps or imbalances in the first three stages, which encompass the ages birth through six years. To plan treatment, we consider the developmental stage at which we suspect the imbalance first occurred. In Frank's case, we guide him in a discussion of what he can remember about that period. There are a multitude of techniques available for use. The therapist may stimulate the client's memory with the use of old photographs or memorabilia from that time period. A small regression chest containing such items is symbolically evocative of the past. The playroom setting aids recall and provides a backdrop against which the adult client can reenact events surrounding the trauma. He or she may be encouraged to play games learned in childhood or to draw pictures of the house lived in at the age of the trauma. The goal is to evoke childhood memories and refamiliarize the client with his or her own development. The client can remember and reexperience feelings that originally caused the disruption in development.

We may also construct or utilize occurrences in therapy to fill in developmental gaps. For example, when I withstood his initial violence and hostility and confronted him with his homosexuality, I demonstrated to Frank that he could trust me. He was fearful, but the balance between trust and mistrust, Erikson's first psychosocial conflict, shifted a bit in favor of trust. He could trust himself to be with me, and trust me to guide him through the exploration of his sexual identity. Clinically, then, developmental theory, taken stage by stage in terms of normal, predictable growth, provides the therapist with more than an understanding of human behavior; it provides charts, maps, and guidelines — a blueprint for treatment. Awareness of this significant factor can motivate a therapist in training to revisit explications of developmental theories with new energy, and new determination to overcome the sometimes dry obscurities of scholastic prose.

To insure maximum impact and durability of outcome in treatment, the words we select should match the level of cognitive development experienced by the client at the time the sexual trauma occurred. This does not mean we engage in baby talk with our clients; rather, we seek the cognitive level of understanding, sorting, and storing of information the child within the client had achieved at the time of the trauma. The goal is to communicate on that level, to access the unexpressed feelings and sensations that are pooled there within the client.

At this point, we open the wound and drain it of its unintegrated matter. The client is guided toward expression of unarticulated reactions to the trauma, in the presence of a supportive and mainly silent therapist.

The symbolic function of the therapist is that of a good parent or caregiver. The child within the client cannot face the terror of reliving the trauma alone. In these moments and throughout the process of therapy, the client draws on a calm strength emanating from the therapist.

Based on Piaget's theory of cognitive development, our gender dysphoric client, Julie (Chapter 8) was capable only of preoperational thought ages two through seven, at the time she was traumatized by the sights and sounds of her parents fighting. Her way of knowing the world and processing information was limited by inability to conceptualize. Developmentally, her thought processes tended to focus on only one aspect of the frightening situation she witnessed, the visualization of her parents' nudity, particularly their genitals. Piaget calls this "centration," a major limitation of preoperational thought. Julie's reasoning and ability to organize the overwhelming stimulation — that is, her nude parents fighting, her awareness of her own small genitals in contrast to their adult genitalia, her father's cursing, and her mother's frightened cries — were limited to a very primitive kind of sorting. The inferences Julie made about what she saw, heard, and felt were confused and incomplete. She was simply unable to process the event. A pool of unexpressed, unarticulated, and thus unintegrated thoughts and emotions was formed and subsequently functioned as an impediment to development. Many years later, in a series of drawings done in a playroom setting, Julie was finally able to sort through what had happened at a level of development symbolically similar to the stage in which the original trauma occurred.

For Julie, the event described above, combined with other traumatic, sexually related incidents, disturbed her development sexually, psychosocially, and cognitively. Sexually, she was gender dysphoric, unable to be female or male for fear she would be either a brutal aggressor, like her father, or a helpless victim, like her mother. Psychosocially, she could not relate successfully with males or females. Cognitively, although she went on to develop subsequent stages of thought, concrete operational (ages seven through eleven), and formal operational (from age eleven on), she experienced extreme confusion and regressed to preoperational thought during times of stress, particularly in situations that related to sexuality or aggression.

Utilization of our knowledge of developmental psychology guides our understanding of the internal state of our clients when they were traumatized. There is also a consequent increase in the therapist's ability to empathize and support clients as they reexperience childhood pain.

Designing the specifics of therapeutic intervention is simplified, since we know how the child felt and what the cognitive processes were at the point of traumatization. Returning to the case of Julie, knowing that she was limited to preoperational thought when she was traumatized and that she was likely to regress to that level of cognition under stress, we approached her therapeutically at a preoperational level in a playroom setting. We encouraged her to draw pictures of what she believed had happened. She drew pictures specifically focused on the trauma. What did Dad look like? What did Mom look like? Her childlike perceptions were accepted without question or comment. It was more important for her to relive the incident as she perceived it than it was for her account to make sense or be totally accurate. If Julie had seen and remembered only genitals, then she is encouraged to draw pictures of what she had seen and the feelings that were engendered by that event.

We can apply our various developmental charts and maps with all clients, regardless of their presenting problem. The charts and maps furnish us with a method of ongoing assessment throughout the therapeutic process. We can cross-validate our assumptions and inferences about client development in all aspects of functioning. Developmental theorists, such as Freud, Erikson, Piaget, and Lawrence Kohler are not mutually exclusive. They provide the basis for scanning client development, both in the present, and retroactively to the point of developmental disruption. We look for stage-level behavior in the psychosexual, psychosocial, cognitive, and moral realms.

When we are concerned with evaluating our client's level of moral development, which is important in treating psychosexual disorder, it is useful to utilize Kohler's three levels of moral development, which are divided predictably into age groups. Level One is preconventional morality (ages four through ten). At this level, we are motivated simply by a desire to avoid punishment and satisfy our own personal needs. At Level Two, conventional morality (ages ten through thirteen), we are motivated by a desire to be liked and to avoid disapproval of established authority figures. Finally, at Level Three, postconventional morality (adolescence to maturity), motivation is decidedly altruistic. The goal is to maintain respect of the community and to obey laws beneficial to the entire community.

Moral development in sexually disturbed people is frequently arrested at the first level. Preconventional morality is characterized by self-centered behaviors and is governed only by the desire to avoid punishment. Toward the end of this stage, which begins at age four and ends with age ten, there is a stage of development that Kohler labels "instrumental-relativist." Simply stated, the child at this level of moral development is motivated only by the desire to satisfy his own needs. Sexual or social impulses are curbed only by the personal need to avoid punishment and satisfy oneself. Right and wrong or the needs of others are not issues of concern.

We, as therapists, have to teach, or "layer in," moral guidelines in a language the client will understand and accept. For example, William, who sexually molested his younger sister, Marie, was twelve years old when he first started to sexually abuse his five-year-old sister (Chapter 9). Since William himself had been sexually molested by a babysitter when he was nine, and had never received treatment or talked about it to anyone, his moral development had been compromised. At the time he entered treatment with me, he was forty years old. He still engaged in an incestuous relationship with his sister, then thirty-three, convinced that their sexual relationship was okay, even healthy. Their presenting problem had nothing to do, in their minds, with the incestuous nature of their relationship. They were concerned only with Marie's sexual sadism and William's sexual masochism, which they sought to control so they could continue to relate sexually.

Incest is not in the best interest of the community. Based on Kohler's levels, we would expect William and Marie, as functioning adults, to be at Level Three of moral development, postconventional morality, in which they would have concern for maintaining social order and obeying laws. Instead, due to the sexual traumatization they both experienced at Level One, preconventional morality, they had failed to complete the developmental stage in which disruption occurred. They had not progressed to even the next level, conventional morality, where they would have been motivated to avoid disapproval of authority figures.

Their moral development was based only on a desire to avoid punishment and satisfy their own needs. William and Marie exemplify Level One in moral development, which is developmentally appropriate for four- to ten-year-olds. This is not uncommon for sexually disturbed people who have been traumatized in early childhood. William had been twelve; Marie, five. Our Eriksonian chart of psychosocial development places them in separate stages. William, at twelve years, should have been developing significant relationships at school or with age-level peers in the neighborhood. The feelings of conflict he had to balance were industry versus infe-

riority. Favorable outcomes for that stage would revolve around social skills and age-level proficiency, physically and intellectually.
Instead of accomplishing those developmental tasks, his energies
were being channeled into an incestuous relationship with his
younger sister. He was forced to function prematurely as a parent,
because his own mother was incompetent and his father was usually absent from the home. William's sexual feelings, which normally would have been less obvious at this age, were in the
forefront of his awareness, to the detriment of resolving the age-
appropriate tasks.

Marie was five years old when the incestuous sexual relationship
complicated the precarious developmental balance she had managed to achieve in the previous, muscular anal stage, one to three
years. At that stage her significant relationships should have been
with her parents, but she had only William to rely on. For Marie
the developmental outcomes were decidedly unfavorable. She
failed to achieve feelings of adequacy and self-control. She could
not assert herself. Instead of developing a balance between autonomy and shame, the Eriksonian psychological task at that point, a
serious imbalance had occurred. Marie felt only shame, without
any sense of autonomy. This was her condition when she was sexually molested by her brother, and her psychosocial development
had been seriously compromised by the resulting trauma. Marie
should have been developing personal initiative and a sense of purpose and direction. This did not occur. Instead, she was controlled
and sexually exploited by her older brother, who had become her
surrogate parent. The appropriate developmental task at age five is
to develop a healthy balance between initiative versus guilt. Instead, guilt predominated.

What were the implications for treatment? We have a clinical decision to make; we could regress the clients, William and Marie, to
the developmental ages at which sexual traumatization had occurred and layer in appropriate behavior, thus targeting the point
when they, as an incestuous pair, first started to relate sexually. Or
we could focus on the present and utilize our developmental data
to modify their current behavior. This alternative was selected because of the urgent need to arrest their sexual sadism and masochism.

Understanding their developmental positions provided a basis for formulating treatment. Due to the nature of the presenting problem, their desire to improve their sexual relationship, individual treatment focused on developmental balance was not indicated. They had to be treated as a couple because of the ongoing incestuous relationship. The immediate point of intervention was the present and their concern about the sexual disorders that were disturbing their relationship. William wanted help with curbing, not eliminating, Marie's sadistic tendencies during their encounters. Both William and Marie suffered from sexual masochism in their current encounters.

I did not utilize the playroom, nor did I engage in a symbolic search of the past. Instead, I helped them clarify their feelings and confront their own behaviors. I was able to accomplish this successfully with the aid of the developmental maps I carried in my head during our sessions. Developmental maps and charts take various forms, depending on the clinician constructing them.

Students and training associates, using this method, frequently sketch out block charts, concentric circles, and/or parallel lines. The significant factor seems to be in the process of thinking about the client developmentally and placing him or her on a growth continuum that approximates stage and age-level outcome, so that treatment can be planned effectively. When therapists utilize this method, they seldom engage in random interventions or waste precious time. The method insures that therapy is planned, and that interventions are targeted and focus on the sexual problem. This approach can be used with all types of presenting problems, but it is essential in the treatment of sexual disturbance, which must be client specific. Specificity is best accomplished through the use of developmental charts and maps, designed for that purpose by the clinician who will be executing the treatment.

Utilizing a developmental blueprint to plan client-specific treatment creates empathic understanding of the sexually disturbed. It is difficult to judge or condemn a client for a sexual crime once its formation is understood. How can one blame or condemn someone for experiencing developmental misfortune?

12
Clinical Presence

The therapeutic presence need not emanate mystical power and authority. Calmness, openness, and responsiveness to feelings generally assure the client that help is available. The sexually disturbed person may initially judge the therapist based on what he or she has grown to expect from past authority figures. He or she may scrutinize the dress and mannerisms of the therapist for signs of sexual bias and attempt to classify or stereotype the therapist sexually. People with sexual secrets who seek therapy are not sure they can be helped. The sexually disturbed person has a great deal to lose if the process is ineffective. The cost includes prolonged suffering, as well as time and money.

At the outset the client may be so distraught by his or her problem that details of the therapeutic presence are not immediately noticed. As therapy continues and deepens, the sexually disturbed client becomes increasingly aware of the therapist as a person, a sexual person. The therapist is thus furnished with an opportunity to utilize his or her total presence as a positive force for healing.

Therapeutic effectiveness is dependent upon many variables. Bringing them together in a smooth and harmonious manner is a combination of art and science. Clinical application of psychological theory through the use of developmental charts and maps is a significant component. The presence and personality of the therapist are equally significant. Therapeutic presence includes such details as self-awareness, dress, voice tone, and overall demeanor. The ability to establish rapport and respond on a feeling level is especially important in the treatment of the sexually disturbed. If the therapist is dressed in a provocative manner, is overly friendly and social, or engages in sexually suggestive behaviors, it is unlikely that therapy will occur. Personal remarks about client appearance or casual touching can create an unforeseen reaction, since the client might easily misunderstand the therapist's intent or meaning. This is particularly true for the sexually disturbed. Rapport is thus damaged. Used appropriately, touch and personal comments can be powerful reinforcers in therapy. They should be conserved for just that purpose.

A word of clarification regarding the meaning of feeling in therapy. Responsiveness to the feelings of the client, and communication of that responsiveness, establishes rapport by giving the client the sense of being understood. Content tends to be less important, with the notable exception of information useful in structuring the developmental charts and maps necessary for treatment planning.

Taking notes during session or involving a client in a paper barricade of data-gathering for insurance purposes, or even for treatment planning, can be an extremely negative experience. Sexual history forms or sexual problem histories are best done either as a take-home assignment or in another room, apart from the counseling chamber. These specifics are best attended to after a feeling-level contact has been established.

Thus, the initial contact between the therapist and the sexually disturbed client is most successful if feelings are allowed to surface. By feeling, we do not mean *therapist* feeling. Warm, fuzzy hugs or overly empathic feeling reflections are not effective. A calm, open, attentive attitude can be communicated nonverbally, with a minimum of nodding and changes in facial expression. The sexually disturbed person, or any anxious or defensive client, will be alert to nongenuine warmth or cognitive detachment, which will make a negative difference in therapeutic outcomes.

Self-disclosure on the part of the therapist generally evokes similar disclosure on the part of the client. This can be useful in therapy, but in treatment of the sexually disturbed, caution must be exercised. With a sexual abuse victim there is a heightened sensitivity to personal closeness. Self-disclosure, or inviting the client into the private world of the therapist, may be perceived by the client as threatening or seductive. Self-disclosure, touch, or other counseling techniques must be used judiciously when working with the sexually disturbed.

Maintaining appropriate boundaries between client and therapist is always important, and boundary setting takes on another dimension when working with a person that has been sexually traumatized. Incestuous families, for example, have difficulty with sexual boundaries. Often the sexually disturbed client has not learned how to set or maintain sexual boundaries between self and others. The therapist has an opportunity, and a responsibility, to teach and model appropriate boundary setting. This applies to the therapist's manner of dress for the counseling setting, personal remarks about client appearance, touch, and self-disclosure. There should be no doubt in the mind of the sexually disturbed client about the limits of the counselor-client relationship. These limits are in addition to the basic injunction against sexual contact between counselor and client. The sexually disturbed person will be likely to feel arousal during sessions, and may fantasize or dream about sexual contact with the therapist. This is a predictable and natural part of working with the sexually disturbed. Because there is so much talk about sex and focus on sex, one begins to feel sexual. This is true for the therapist as well as the client. As in working with other clients, sexual arousal on the part of the client can be acknowledged and talked about. Therapist arousal toward the client is best not mentioned. The sexually disturbed client could easily misunderstand the therapist's motivation in mentioning it. If the client asks whether the therapist is sexually attracted to him or her, a therapeutic lie is generally in order. Being open and honest is not always therapeutically sound. Counselors who seek to reassure a client that he or she is sexually attractive should guard against using personal interest for reassurance purposes. With the sexually disturbed client, it is necessary to clarify the process of setting sexual boundaries and encourage the client to take part in the process, so sexual boundary setting will be easier for him or her in the future. Commenting on the process of therapy, what you are doing and why you are doing it, serves as an internal summary for the client and keeps therapeutic goals in sight.

As in most therapy, there is a great deal of repetition in teaching new behaviors. It is rarely sufficient to make a point only once in the course of therapy. Take sexual boundary setting, for example, as in the case of Loretta, who suffered from incestuous pedophilia, nonexclusive type (Chapter 6). We can trace her difficulty in setting sexual boundaries with her own son, as well as her indiscriminate sexual response with men and women, directly to her father's failure to set sexual boundaries with her. We clarified in session that this was a serious problem, one that Loretta could well pass along to her own son if she did not set firm sexual boundaries for her nuclear family and stay within those boundaries. We drew her spouse into the process, and there was a strong awareness in the family that we were working to establish stable sexual boundaries.

Whenever an issue regarding the counselor-client relationship emerged, such as Loretta's sexual fantasies about having a relationship with me, I was very clear that her feelings toward me were normal and predictable and that there wasn't even the faintest possibility that we would ever relate sexually or even socially. She was disappointed, but felt a great deal of relief that I consistently maintained appropriate boundaries in our relationship. I thus modeled and taught her that sexual boundary setting was possible, positive, and appropriate. As a result she was able to alter her own previously indiscriminate sexual behavior and successfully set sexual boundaries in her own life. While it is always necessary to set clear boundaries between therapist and client regarding social and sexual contact, this is especially true with the sexually disturbed. There is always the possibility that an ill-trained or unaware therapist will compound rather than heal the emotional wound experienced by the client.

Psychological defenses are necessary and healthy. They protect us from pain and help us organize our perceptions. They also protect the client from therapy and the therapist from knowledge of self.

Self-awareness is comprised of knowledge of one's own defense system. A therapist who is uncomfortable with feelings will often guide the client away from in-depth exploration of feelings or will collude with a cognitively oriented client to focus on content rather than underlying feeling. While much of sexual counseling is content specific and involves behavioral components, as in the treatment of erectile or ejaculatory dysfunction in the male or of preorgasmia and vaginismus in the female, it is paramount that the therapist be able to guide the client in the discussion of feelings evoked by the treatment process. If, as is frequently the case, the therapist has unresolved sexual issues, it may be difficult to separate therapist sexual concerns from those of the sexually disturbed client. This may result in focus on therapist rather than client sexual issues. Or there may be no focus at all on either sexual issues or feelings.

There are many useful discussions of the defense system and how it works. Seminal work done by Sigmund Freud, enlarged upon by Anna Freud and Karen Horney, are excellent sources. Clinical application requires much more than familiarity with the meaning of terms such as projection, attributing our own desires and impulses to others, or denial, refusal to admit the truth. Most therapists have memorized the terms and can build on that knowledge to understand how these various mechanisms can be used to facilitate rather than impede therapy.

At the outset of each client's therapy, the therapist analyzes his or her own defenses. This procedure becomes a model for understanding client defenses. Since ego defenses are habitual and usually unconscious, even a seasoned therapist must augment his or her own analyses with external sources. Probably the most expedient method is to seek this information from a colleague who has known the therapist over time and observed him or her doing therapy. It is also extremely useful to assess the defense mechanisms commonly used by members of the therapist's family of origin, as we frequently imitate behaviors we are exposed to as children.

Suppose that denial is a main defense. Denial can be defined simply as refusal to admit the truth. Denial takes many forms, from not accepting an obvious truth, like the loss of a loved one, to the existence of anger toward a parent or spouse. This level of denial may be outside of conscious awareness. Denial also permits escape from anxiety on a semiconscious level. Unpleasant thoughts and realities are screened out. For a clinician, this may even result in failure to acknowledge ineffectiveness in clinical work. These failures are commonly due to intolerance of emotional pain in self or clients. Another frequent form of denial is the failure to recognize, in the therapeutic setting, that a client is ready to terminate therapy. Therapist motivation, for contact or income, may prolong therapy beyond the point of usefulness.

Unfortunately, a therapist can experience both levels of denial, conscious and unconscious, simultaneously with the same client. Supervision, self, peer, or otherwise, is usually sufficient to identify and remedy this type of therapist denial. At a more subtle level, denial can cause therapist avoidance of subject areas that are personally unpleasant or distasteful. In working with the sexually disturbed, many distasteful events must be discussed and explored in depth. This may be painful and embarrassing for the client, who may also employ denial to avoid facing the truth. The therapist who is aware of his or her own use of denial as a defense mechanism can compensate by evaluating each session for telltale signs of denial or avoidance.

After clarifying and reviewing one's own defense system and how it works, the therapist evaluates the defense system of the sexually disturbed client. This can be accomplished by attending carefully to the communication style, body language, and attendant mannerisms of the client in the course of therapy. Does the client smile to conceal anger, change the subject when a sensitive issue is approached, feign confusion when painful material is presented, blame the therapist or significant others to avoid taking responsibility, talk about painful experiences in an intellectual manner to avoid feeling pain?

Listing client defenses is an important part of treatment planning. Once this is done, the therapist can compare his or her own defenses to those of the sexually disturbed client. Similar defenses can create problems in therapy, but therapist awareness can prevent unnecessary enmeshment of the two defense systems. Remembering that we all make adjustive reactions to protect ourselves from loss of self-esteem, guilt, or anxiety will aid the clinician in avoiding enmeshment in his own and client defenses during the course of therapy.

Basic defense systems are usually covered in any undergraduate psychology text. Recognizing the function of defense systems and how they are manifested in therapy supplies the therapist with increased ability to heal. Only the therapist who knows and understands his or her own defense system is equipped to guide a sexually disturbed client beyond self-deception and distortion of reality. Recognizing defensive behavior in a client is for the most part easier than recognizing it in oneself.

Intensity of response is a major indicator of defensive behavior. In the case of Frank (Chapter 7), involving ego dystonic homosexuality, we see a rigid overuse of denial. His shouting, threatening, aggressive overreaction illustrates the intensity of a neurotic defense. He could not face his homosexuality directly and deal with it rationally. He desperately sought to avoid the reality of his sexual identity by marrying a woman to whom he was not sexually attracted, fathering a child, and engaging in chauvinistic womanizing. His neurotic defenses continued to be unsuccessful in staving off anxiety and banishing his erotic sexual impulses toward males. The overuse of denial involved such a high degree of self-deception and distortion of reality that he simply could not make it work, and he remained anxious. Indicators of his defensive behaviors were their intensity, rigidity, and overuse.

Defense systems, whether healthy or neurotic, clinician or client, can be identified and circumvented in the therapeutic setting. Once a therapist is aware of his own commonly used psychological defenses and the more extreme forms they take in the sexually disturbed client, much ineffective therapy is avoided.

A word about clinical presence in working with the sexually disturbed client. Sexual self-awareness, or self-knowledge about one's own sexuality, is essential. A therapist who has been sexually abused, and is working with a client who has had a similar experience, must be cognizant of the inherent danger of confusing the circumstances of the client's abuse with those of his or her own.

Sexual preferences, disapproval of particular types of sexual stimulation, or positioning during sexual encounters can easily be imposed on a client while talking about the client's sexual behaviors. Therapist bias can be avoided only if the therapist has thoroughly assessed his or her own sexual likes and dislikes and has developed a habitual openness to the diversity of sexual orientation and behavior that exists in the normal population. This does not imply the sanctioning of abnormal sexual behavior, particularly as it relates to the harming of self or others. The implication is rather that any hint of judgment or disapproval of sexual acts that one might not personally engage in, such as anal sex or bondage, is withheld. Ideally, such judgment would not be felt, but it is a rare therapist who does not feel some judgment or disapproval while counseling the sexually disturbed. When the client senses the disapproval, rapport is damaged. This happens more often in working with the sexually disturbed client than it does with clients who present with other types of problems. The sexually disturbed client cannot be healed if acceptance of his sexual nature is withheld. Without acceptance, the process of therapy will falter.

13
Client Humanity

Dehumanization of the sexually disturbed is a serious clinical problem. In gathering the information we need to plan treatment, we may overgeneralize the nature of their sexual disorder and fail to understand how unique each sexually disturbed person really is. As a result, the therapy is less precise. An element of desensitization occurs when a therapist in training reads about the essential features of psychosexual disorders. As we become familiar with the frequency of occurrences, sex ratio, and what is known about predisposing factors of the specific sexual disturbances, we are better able to plan and deliver treatment to our sexually disturbed clients.

Material drawn from the *Diagnostic and Statistical Manual of Mental Disorders* (DSM-III, 1980; DSM-III-R, 1987) furnishes guidelines for basic understanding of the sexually disturbed. The various disorders suffered by the sexually disturbed are coded statistically for communication purposes, and the classifications are consistently revised to reflect changing knowledge and political conditions. For example, the diagnosis "ego dystonic homosexuality," which describes the condition experienced by Frank (Chapter 7), appeared in DSM-III (1980). However, the DSM-III-R (1987) eliminated this diagnostic category, and Frank's diagnosis became "other sexual disorders." Although this category is less precise, the condition remains the same. Frank could not accept his homosexual arousal response and sought instead to strengthen his weak heterosexual arousal response. His same-sex arousal response persisted, even though Frank did not want it to be part of him. The revised *Diagnostic and Statistical Manual* lists Frank's essential characteristics as marked feelings of inadequacy concerning his self-imposed standards of masculinity, marked distress about his sexual orientation, and a pattern of sexual conquests with people who only existed for him as things to be used. Although the statistical classification by which Frank would be diagnosed changed, the essential features remained the same. The change seems to reflect political rather than clinical change.

It is helpful to think of the sexually disturbed in broad categories, such as paraphiliac psychosexual dysfunctions, gender identity disorders, and other unspecified psychosexual disorders. It is important to remember that the purpose of classification is not to dehumanize the sexually disturbed client but to gain information useful in understanding the client and planning effective treatment.

A therapist can acquire a working knowledge of psychosexual disorders by becoming familiar with pertinent sections of the *Diagnostic and Statistical Manual,* but when it comes to application of that knowledge, it is clear that each sexually disturbed person must also be evaluated in terms of how he or she differs from the clinical descriptions of the specific disorder; differences as well as similarities guide us in treatment planning. As with the use of developmental charts and analyses of defense systems, we use the data to make our approach more specific, and more personal, to the sexually disturbed person we seek to help.

Intense recurrent sexual urges and fantasies that are not part of a normative arousal response affect each sexually disturbed person differently. When working with a client who has been sexually traumatized, it is useful to evaluate the disorder in terms of its intensity. Severe, moderate, or mild levels of the same sexual disorder yield to different therapeutic approaches.

Roy, the homosexual pedophiliac (Chapter 10), repeatedly acted on his impulses and sexually molested young boys in the same way that he himself had been sexually molested as a child. His disturbance was severe and would yield only to intense, long-term regression therapy that targeted the developmental problem, combined with a shorter-term behavioral approach directed at the acting-out behavior.

Loretta, who had been victimized by her father (Chapter 6), an incestuous pedophiliac, developed a moderate case of incestuous pedophilia herself. Her feelings were as intense and recurring as those experienced by Roy, but she acted on them only once or twice as a child and successfully overcame them, although her feelings continued throughout her adolescence and young adulthood. With the aid of light regression therapy she shifted from a moderate to a mild level of sexual disturbance. Like many paraphiliacs, she was plagued by an indiscriminate sexual response to both males and females. Although she did not consistently act on these feelings, they caused her extreme distress and hampered her ability to sustain a relationship with her husband. Her treatment involved conjoint sessions with her spouse, as well as sessions involving her family of origin.

The term paraphilia relates to deviant (para) attraction (philia). Loretta had three or four paraphilias, which is not uncommon. Neither she nor Roy had other mental disorders, but in working with the sexually disturbed we do find that they often suffer concurrently from substance abuse or personality disorder.

Another broad term, gender identity disorder, relates primarily to individuals who feel extreme discomfort with their anatomic sex and their gender identity. Ben, the transsexual (Chapter 5), reported feeling like a woman encapsulated in a man's body. His sexual disturbance took several forms throughout his life span. As a child, when he played "dress up" and wore his mother's clothes, he had felt like a girl, not a boy. In his private world he imagined himself to be female, so much so that he was uncomfortable with his assigned sex and had a definite sense of being female. Ben's gender identity had its inception in childhood. Before he reached puberty, he developed the habit of urinating sitting down on the toilet instead of adopting the male standing position. He had many of the other characteristics of gender identity disorder of childhood, including disgust with his penis and testicles, and an aversion to sports and rough play. Although almost one-third of male children with this disorder develop a homosexual identity postpubescence, this was not the case with Ben. He did, however, go through a period of transvestic fetishism before he reached an adult conclusion that he was transsexual. Although he functioned as a conservative businessman, he maintained a collection of women's clothes and makeup, with which he transformed himself, masturbated, and fantasized that males were attracted to him as a woman. As in most cases of transvestic fetishism, Ben was basically heterosexual until later in life, when he made a choice to enter a homosexual relationship and live out his life as a transsexual who did not seek surgical sexual reassignment.

In retrospect, we trace his gender identity disorder back to childhood and through a continuum that included a period of time as a heterosexual transvestite, until he developed into a transsexual homosexual. This progression is not unusual. Julie (Chapter 8) was classified as gender identity disorder of adolescence or adulthood nontranssexual (GIDAANT). This too had its inception in childhood, when she was sexually traumatized by observing her nude parents fighting. Later she was sexually abused by her father and developed an unusual paraphiliac condition, involving alternate attraction to females and males, mixed with sexual aversion. As a young adult she assumed a modified lesbian identity, which with the help of regression therapy yielded to a heterosexual identity.

Like Ben, the transsexual, Julie's gender identity disorder followed a continuum from childhood through adolescence and adulthood. Although Julie cross-dressed, which is considered less of a disorder for females, wearing male attire did not cause sexual excitement for her; thus she was never classified as a transvestic fetishist. This classification seems to be reserved for males in the diagnostic criteria of the DSM-III-R (1987), which seems inaccurate, at least in my experience. Many females report sexually arousing fantasies when dressed in male clothing. Perhaps this classification, as with others, will change with time.

Sexual exhibitionism usually occurs in males, but our culture encourages women to exhibit themselves in so many provocative ways that this disorder may be passed over or remain undiagnosed in females. In the case of Annie (Chapter 4), sexual exhibitionism resulted from imitating her father, who exposed his genitals to Annie's mother and masturbated himself in the child's presence. Annie herself became an exhibitionist and exposed her genitals to both males and females, acting on recurrent, intense sexual urges to startle or shock her victims. She imagined that her victims would be aroused by the sight of her genitals, as she herself was when she recalled her father masturbating himself in front of her when she was a child.

Generally, the feelings experienced by the sexually disturbed, whether they are broadly classified as paraphiliac or as gender identity disorders, are intense, recurrent, and very difficult to resist. Thus it is not unusual for a sexual dysfunction to occur as a result of the stress involved in having one or more of the paraphilias or a gender identity disorder. The physiologic changes that characterize the sexual response cycle are inhibited, and the individual may be unable to achieve normal erection, ejaculation, arousal, or orgasm. Pain may also be present, as in the case of dyspareunia or vaginismus. A behavioral approach to these conditions in the sexually disturbed will not be effective without concurrent, deeper-level intervention. Therapy must focus on the underlying cause, as well as on the symptoms. The emotional issues surrounding the treatment of sexual dysfunction must also be explored. The sexually disturbed person must be encouraged to talk about reactions to the therapist and to the process of therapy.

Therapy itself can be a traumatic experience. There is much pain in reliving childhood sexual trauma. It is extremely difficult for people to talk about their sexual behavior in explicit terms. To do so is to violate social and cultural prohibitions. Since many sexually disturbed people have been traumatized by members of their families or by close family friends, they also experience feelings of disloyalty and shame regarding their family of origin. It is difficult not to respect the sexually disturbed who seek therapy and struggle through the pain required for healing. Again, the main factor in successful treatment is the attitude of the therapist: recognizing and respecting the humanity of the sexually disturbed person.

14
Curative Powers in Therapy

The curative power, or healing agent, lies within the client with the psychosexual disturbance. The therapist acts as a guide. Confused mislearning and unexpressed feelings within the sexually disturbed person need exploration and reordering. If an original event or series of events occurred that interrupted the course of normal sexual development, the event must be clarified and understood. Only then can any semblance of normal sexual development and functioning be resumed.

In order to approach and resolve these painful sexual disturbances, the client must feel safety. Most sexually disturbed people are overwhelmed with fear at the outset of therapy. The therapist responds with reassurance and support. Accustomed to negative biases against their sexual disturbances, the sexually disturbed do not usually expect to be liked or accepted. They conceal negative self-evaluation. In fact, if the therapist generates nongenuine liking and respect, the sexually disturbed person will respond with disbelief, mistrust, and anxiety. It is unlikely that therapy will occur. More significantly, the already damaged client will be negatively affected by exposure to professional hypocrisy.

Most therapists don't like people with psychosexual disorders. This is understandable. It is hard to like someone who has committed a sexual crime against a child, or who needs to inflict pain on an unwilling partner to feel sexual arousal. Therapist distaste for deviant sexual behavior is a barrier to successful treatment. When I look at the limited success rate in the treatment of psychosexual disorder, I wonder whether it is a function of the chronicity of the disorder or of a lack of commitment, persistence, and good will on the part of the therapist. It is difficult to feel good will when the negative reaction to the deviant sexual behavior is so easily generalized to the person.

The disgust felt for child molestation readily becomes disgust with the child molester. Seeing the perpetrator as a former victim may not be enough, because our perception of victims is often limited to pity, not understanding. Pity is not therapeutic. The difficult task for the therapist is to discriminate between an unacceptable behavior and an acceptable person. Therapists must separate their reaction to the behavior from their reaction to the sexually disturbed person.

Most of the work is done by the client. If the therapist is reasonably well-trained at the master's or doctoral level, has a working knowledge of applied psychological theory, and is familiar with psychosexual disorder, therapeutic success is within reach. Leading the client through the confusion and pain to the point of psychological encounter, where healing can occur, requires sexual self-knowledge on the part of the therapist. It is easy to choose avoidance of pain, client pain and therapist pain, by working at a superficial level. A curative force in the treatment of psychosexual disorder is the recurrence of intense feeling at appropriate moments. This is because sexual disturbance, which we will call a disruption in normal sexual development, is caused by and associated with intense emotion. When the sexually disturbed person approaches the sensitive area, the memory of the original pain and/or confusion returns. Sometimes it is mingled with erotic sensations, but the predominant feeling is fear, fear of the emotion, fear of the memory. If the therapist also becomes fearful and interrupts the process, healing does not occur. If the therapist can remain silent and let the client experience the pain and make some sense of it, healing generally occurs. The calm presence of the therapist encourages the sexually disturbed person to regress into the past and express the feelings and verbalize the thoughts that gave rise to the aberrant behavior. This is a slow process. It involves patience and time similar to reparenting.

A safe regression into the past and a safe return to the present is a healing experience. The sexually disturbed person, accompanied by the therapist, talks about and recalls past sexual feelings, thoughts, and events, sorting them into understandable and more acceptable form. Trauma is soothed. New learning that approximates normal sexual development replaces the distorted and deviant mislearning that first caused the sexual disturbance. The therapist listens, clarifies, and confronts as needed. The sharing of the total experience, as it is perceived by the client, and the quiet acceptance of the therapist constitute a curative element.

Much of the work is symbolic. Setting is important. If the sessions take place in a playroom, a nursery, or an adolescent rap room, symbolizing return to the past, it is easier for the sexually disturbed person to recall and reorder past learning. These settings are most effective if they are suggestive in nature, with little clutter to distract the regressed client from his or her own personal remembrance. The therapist, utilizing the transference, permits the client to express anger, resentment, shame, guilt, and all other feelings that are evoked by the symbolic reenactment of the past. Steadfast compliance with ethical and professional guidelines is essential if the sexually disturbed client is to learn appropriate sexual boundaries and recover from the psychosexual disturbance.

No sexual touch occurs between client and therapist. The element of transference, which aids the sexually disturbed person in returning to the past to reorder sexual mislearning, also renders the client helpless in the presence of the therapist. This vulnerability approximates the plight of the child victim of sexual crime and/or the child state at the point of mislearning. The therapist must therefore act with extreme caution and sexual self-awareness.

The sexually disturbed person is open to new learning at this point. This does not imply that the sexual values of the therapist are imposed. Rather, the absence or removal of the negative value or behavior constitutes appropriate learning. Calm silence and avoidance of touch that could be misconstrued by the sexually disturbed client is essential.

The therapist may experience sexual arousal, which is particularly common if the therapist is not accustomed to working with erotic material. Refocusing on the needs of the client while remaining silent and still is sufficient to maintain therapy. So long as the therapist does not act on these feelings or allow them to become a distraction, they will not impede therapeutic progress.

There is a mystical quality that enables the therapist to transcend his or her own sexual biases and values and enter the inner world of the sexually disturbed person. Judgmental attitudes slip away, and the therapist truly knows what the client is experiencing. The attention, contact, commitment, and purposeful presence of the therapist activates the process of healing.

This empathy, or joining, approximates a momentary blending of identities. This is imperfectly described as spiritual. The sexually disturbed person feels this mystical component as acceptance, forgiveness, or whatever is needed to activate the process of healing. The outrage and violation that interrupted normal sexual development and resulted in mislearning are countered. Developmental balance is restored. A rough approximation of normal sexual development will follow.

What is this mystical element? The simultaneously felt poignancy assures the client that he or she is being cared for and protected. The feeling is generalized as the longed-for parental love and protection missing at the time of the trauma or mislearning. This time, the generalization is remedial. Detoxification occurs, and the emotional valance of the disturbing sexual event is mitigated. The therapeutic relationship fills in the gap. Energized by this feeling, the sexually disturbed person cognitively reframes the mislearning, or original sexual trauma, as less significant and sees himself or herself as capable of normal functioning. The deviant act no longer has to be repeated. The anxiety that drives the compulsion has dissipated. The experience has been integrated. The psychosexual disorder is eventually replaced with a close approximation of normal sexual functioning.

15
Regression: Access to the Pockets of the Mind

The course of normal sexual development is dependent upon what a child experiences within the family context. Although many children experience sexual trauma perpetrated by nonfamily members, and much sexual mislearning occurs outside the family, the sexual attitudes and behaviors operating within the family system frequently have the power either to compound the deleterious effects of sexual trauma or to ameliorate the sexual mislearning. In some cases the child is able to talk about and express feelings arising from the event. This makes it more likely that a semblance of normal sexual development will occur. Understanding the perceptions that the sexually disturbed person has formed of family members when he or she was a child illuminates his or her view of family sexuality, as well as his or her own sexual self-esteem. Moreover, when a sexual trauma occurs, the manner in which it is treated by family members determines the amount of damage done to the child. Unfortunately, the vast majority of these incidents are handled incorrectly, resulting in a disturbance that has lasting impact on the child's sexual development.

While regression therapy with the sexually disturbed does not always include actual sessions with the family members, it is rarely effective without knowledge of the family members and their sexual identities, as perceived by the sexually disturbed person. Changes in that perception are likely to occur throughout the course of therapy. This information can be gathered in a variety of ways, depending on the client and the skill of the therapist. Sexual histories and questionnaires are rarely helpful when done in session. They distract from the personal nature of the relationship between the therapist and the person with the psychosexual disorder. Therapists who are most comfortable taking notes during sessions rather than making direct eye contact with the sexually disturbed client are best suited for other types of therapy.

The sexually disturbed person has a better chance of resolving the psychosexual disorder by returning to the past within the safety of a therapeutic relationship. Recalling and reframing the incident symbolically is the goal. The release of unexpressed emotion facilitates healing.

Regression therapy can be done at various levels of intensity. Light regression work can occur in a conventional office setting using simple methods. Annie, the sexual exhibitionist (Chapter 4), and Frank, the ego dystonic homosexual (Chapter 7), are examples. The sexually disturbed person can be encouraged to look at photographs of self as a child, or draw pictures of the house or bedroom where the perceptions were formed. I have noticed that many sexually disturbed people have been helped to recall old sexual feelings and perceptions by drawing sketches of the bathrooms they used in early childhood. This seems to bring back early childhood associations of sexuality or sexual events, which frequently involve urination and defecation.

Deeper-level regression of the sexually disturbed person frequently involves reviewing baby books and retrieving old toys. If no relics of the past remain, the sexually disturbed person is encouraged to browse through infant wear and accessories for babies available in department and drug stores. Even selecting a baby blanket one "would have liked to have had" starts a symbolic regression to infancy and early childhood. Deeper levels of regression occur only after the transference has been developed and trust between the sexually disturbed client and the therapist has been established. Julie, the case of gender dysphoria (Chapter 8), and Roy, the homosexual pedophiliac (Chapter 10), are cases in point. Usually it is necessary to make a symbolic journey to the past several times, to sort through the feelings and clarify the thoughts clustered around the disturbance.

Symbolically taking a sexually disturbed client back to the developmental period where sexual mislearning occurred makes it possible for the disturbed person to reexperience the event within the original psychological context. That is to say, the client can emotionally relive the trauma and divest it of its destructive force. This is done with the support of the therapist and of the client's own adult ability to perceive and rethink the original incident.

It is not unusual for a sexually disturbed person to conclude, after a regression experience, that the emotion-laden sexual trauma did not really occur as it was originally remembered. The childish perception, however, did give rise to feelings and beliefs that mingled with sexual sensations and disrupted normal sexual development. Regression therapy is not aimed at establishing the truth or falsehood of the memories from the point of view of the therapist. Regression therapy permits the sexually disturbed person to clarify sexual thoughts and express sexual feelings that were compressed and stored in a pocket of the mind because the child was unable to integrate the experience when it occurred.

The symbolic journey to the past is undertaken to alleviate the effects of fear, shame, anxiety, and guilt on the sexually disturbed. I remind myself of that when I see how much pain it causes a person with a psychosexual disorder to relive the trauma. Is it worth it? This query can be answered only by the sexually disturbed. To willingly undertake a difficult and painful task must mean that the anguish caused by the deviant sexual behavior is more difficult to endure.

In-depth regression therapy is not a brief experience. It usually takes one to three years, with weekly sessions. An intense relationship between the sexually disturbed client and the therapist is formed. When the regression is completed, the client's sexual behaviors change. Termination is sometimes abrupt. The sexually disturbed person feels less disturbed and is no longer driven to seek therapy to overcome anxiety and sexual frustration. Like a child who no longer needs parenting, the client outgrows the therapeutic relationship. He or she forgets the details of the regression experience. It recedes into the past along with the disturbed behavior. As the childhood mislearning fades, so does the memory of the therapeutic regression experience. The intensity of the transference and attachment to the therapist also fade. The abruptness of termination indicates that the sexually disturbed person is freed from the past and is proceeding toward more normal sexual adjustment.

Glossary

These terms are defined according to the meaning ascribed to them in this book.

Abreaction. Expression of a repressed emotion. This release of unintegrated affect is synonymous with catharsis.

Acting-out. Performance, usually under stress, of behavior learned from another situation. Expression of repressed impulses, the manifest behavior often symbolic of earlier stages in development.

Affect. A synonym for feeling or emotion that expresses an emotional state or reaction.

Ambiguity. Lack of clarity. Possibility that an event or feeling can evoke more than one response.

Ambivalence. Uncertainty. Being attracted to and repelled by mutually exclusive points simultaneously.

Androgyny. Having psychological characteristics or qualities of both sexes.

Anxiety. Feeling of dread and apprehension, sometimes without a specific or realistic cause.

Association. Recurring relationship between psychological phenomena based on prior learning.

Associative attribute. An evocative attribute of memory. Consists of items to which that memory is linked associatively in place or time. Returning to the family home may facilitate the recall of memories that have been forgotten.

Attitude. A lasting characteristic that predisposes us to react in a particular way toward others, things, or ideas. Attitudes are made up of feelings, thoughts, and behaviors.

Aversive therapy. A technique that pairs unpleasant (aversive) stimuli with inappropriate behavior, the goal of which is to evoke negative associations with the inappropriate behavior.

Basic anxiety. Underlying anxiety that arises out of helplessness and insecurity and has its inception in childhood.

Behavior disorder. A socially unacceptable behavior, categorized as pathological. A general term referring to one of the various categories of psychopathology.

Body language. Nonverbal expression of an internal state, often preconscious. Includes facial expression, body posture, and mannerisms.

Cognitive dissonance. An uncomfortable psychological conflict between beliefs, or an incongruence between new information and prior knowledge.

Compensation. Engaging in a behavior or trait to cancel out or cover up a deficiency in another area. Can be an unconscious act that generates an alternate behavior for the purpose of relieving anxiety.

Compulsion. Repetitive act or activity aimed at controlling anxiety or satisfying an obsession.

Context. Conditions surrounding a process which affect or alter the meaning of a thought, feeling, or behavior.

Counterconditioning. The weakening or elimination of a learned response by learning a new response stronger than the original. In therapy, it replaces unacceptable feelings, thoughts, and behaviors with acceptable ones.

Defense mechanisms. An unconscious, anxiety-reducing process by which an individual protects himself from pain or unpleasant truth.

Denial. Failure to see or admit truth. Minimization of a situation or event to avoid unacceptable feelings.

Desensitization. A process in which responses are reconditioned so that previously unacceptable thoughts and feelings no longer elicit anxiety.

Developmental Psychology. The organization of human growth that delineates principles of behavioral change in sequential stages from conception to death.

Deviance. Departure from cultural norms regarding what is appropriate and acceptable.

Discrimination. Process of recognizing and differentiating between similar and different aspects of a situation or event.

Emotion. A feeling state such as love, anguish, anger, desire, fear, or shame.

Emotional meaning. Cognitive or feeling associations with a term or symbol beyond its usual referential meaning.

Empathy. A pervasive process that occurs through sensing the emotional state of another.

Fantasy. Imagining of an event, real or otherwise, in concrete symbols or images. Can be pleasant or fearful.

Fixation. A point at which development is suspended. Sequential stages are disrupted or adversely affected.

Forgetting. Inability to recall memory of an event or occurrence.

Generalization. The application, often erroneous, of a response to a large group rather than to a single individual or situation.

Imitation. A fundamental learning process. Patterning one's actions after those of another.

Incongruence. Behavior that is not in line with feeling. Creates confusion, anxiety, or psychological pain.

Integration. A process by which emotions and cognitions are unified in a harmonious manner.

Internalization. A process by which beliefs and behaviors become intrinsic to an individual without external presentation or support.

Latent learning. Learning that appears to occur in the absence of reinforcement, predisposing a person toward a specific reaction in a given context.

Modeling. Social learning in which one imitates the actions or reactions of others.

Motivated forgetting. Forgetting due to a desire to avoid painful memories. Events are distorted or repressed.

Mysticism. A spiritual belief that is not apparent. Sometimes seen as irrational.

Obsession. A persistent feeling, thought, or behavior, often unwanted, associated with anxiety. It recurs and cannot be dismissed by an individual.

Parataxic distortion. Transference of an attitude based on fantasy or on faulty association of a person with other figures.

Perception. A view acquired through sensory receptors and interpretation of information. Based on prior experience as well as on incoming data.

Peripheral learning. The learning of a behavior or association that is in the periphery of the perception, rather than central.

Regression. Psychological return to a previous age level in thought, feeling, and behavior. Can be induced therapeutically, or may occur spontaneously in response to stress.

Repressed emotions. Emotion without consciousness. The existence of such unconscious emotions can be inferred through indirect means, as by mannerisms, facial expressions, or voice tones.

Self. The conscious being, revealed through introspection. A consistent core of psychological process.

Sensation. A simple form of experience perceived through a sense organ.

Sexual mislearning. Sexual learning that interferes with normal sexual development and forms the basis for psychosexual disorder. It can compound and reinforce the negative impact of an existing sexual trauma.

Social learning theory. The assumption that personality is learned and behaviors are based on imitation.

Transference. The stage of therapy in which the client responds to the therapist as though the therapist were some significant person in the client's past or present life (parent, sibling, or spouse).

Trauma. Damage that interrupts normal development and inflicts sustained injury.

Unlearning. Interfering or erasing prior learning by dissolving inappropriate earlier associations and deliberately layering in more acceptable ones.

Selected Bibliography

Allgeier, E. R., and McCormick, N. B. *Changing Boundaries: Gender Roles and Sexual Behavior.* Palo Alto, Calif.: Mayfield, 1983.

Bandura, A. D. "Modeling Approaches to the Modification of Phobic Disorders." *Civa Foundation Symposium: The Role of Learning in Psychotherapy.* London: Churchill, 1968.

———. *Principles of Behavior Modification.* New York: Holt, Rinehart & Winston, 1969.

———. "Psychotherapy Based on Modeling Principles." In *Handbook of Psychotherapy and Behavior Changes,* edited by A. E. Bergin and S. L. Garfield. New York: Wiley, 1971.

———. *Social Learning Theory.* Englewood Cliffs, N.J.: Prentice-Hall, 1977.

Bandura, A., and Menlove, F. "Factors Determining Vicarious Extinction of Avoidance Behavior through Symbolic Modeling." *Journal of Personality and Social Psychology* 8 (1968): 99–108.

Bell, A. P., and Weinberg, M. S. *Homosexualities.* New York: Simon & Schuster, 1978.

Brenton, M. *The American Male.* New York: Coward-McCann, 1966.

Buber, M. *I and Thou.* Trans. W. Kaufmann. New York: Scribner's, 1970.

Coles, R. *Erik H. Erikson: The Growth of His Work.* Boston: Little, Brown, 1970.

Diagnostic and Statistical Manual of Mental Disorders. 3d ed. (DSM-III). Washington, D.C.: American Psychiatric Association, 1980.

Diagnostic and Statistical Manual of Mental Disorders. 3d ed. rev. (DSM-III-R). Washington, D.C.: American Psychiatric Association, 1987.

Dollard, J., and Miller, N. E. *Frustration and Aggression.* New Haven: Yale University Press, 1939.

———. *Social Learning and Imitation.* New Haven: Yale University Press, 1941.

———. *Personality and Psychotherapy.* New York: McGraw-Hill, 1950.

Erikson, E. H. *Childhood and Society.* 2d ed. New York: Norton, 1953.

———. *Insight and Responsibility.* New York: Norton, 1964.

———. *Identity: Youth and Crisis.* New York: Norton, 1968.

———. "Life Cycle." In *International Encyclopedia of the Social Sciences,* vol. 9. New York: Macmillan, 1968.

———. "Psychosocial Identity." In *International Encyclopedia of the Social Sciences,* vol. 7. New York: Macmillan, 1968.

———. *Dimensions of a New Identity.* New York: Norton, 1974.

———. *Toys and Reasons.* New York: Norton, 1977.

———. *Identity and the Life Cycle.* New York: Norton, 1980.

———. *The Life Cycle Completed.* New York: Norton, 1982.

Freud, A. *The Ego and the Mechanisms of Defense.* London: Hogarth, 1937.

Freud, S. *The Psychopathology of Everyday Life.* New York: Norton, 1971.

———. *Inhibitions, Symptoms and Anxiety.* New York: Norton, 1977.

———. *Three Essays on the Theory of Sexuality.* New York: Basic Books, 1982.

———. *The Joke and Its Relation to the Unconscious.* New York: Norton, 1990.

———. *Beyond the Pleasure Principle.* New York: Norton, 1990.

Freud, S., and Breuer, J. *Studies in Hysteria. Standard Edition of Complete Psychological Works of Sigmund Freud,* vol. 2. London: Hogarth, 1955.

Horney, K. *The Neurotic Personality of Our Time.* New York: Norton, 1937.

———. *New Ways in Psychoanalysis.* New York: Norton, 1939.

———. *Neurosis and Human Growth.* New York: Norton, 1950.

Kohler, L. "State and Sequence: The Cognitive Developmental Approach to Socialization." In *Handbook of Socialization and Research,* edited by D. S. Goslin. Chicago: Rand McNally, 1969.

Minuchen, S. *Families and Family Therapy.* Cambridge: Harvard University Press, 1974.

Minuchen, S., and Fishman, H. C. *Family Therapy Techniques.* Cambridge: Harvard University Press, 1981.

Moreno, J. L. *Psychodrama.* Boston: Beacon, 1969.

Index

ABOUT THE AUTHOR

AVERIL MARIE DOYLE is a psychotherapist with more than twenty years' experience as a clinician, specializing in human sexuality and family dynamics. She is a national supervisor for the American Association of Sex Educators, Counselors, and Therapists and is a clinical supervisor for the American Board of Sexology. She is a national supervisor for the American Association of Marriage and Family Therapists. Dr. Doyle has taught graduate courses in human sexuality and sex therapy for medical students and counselors. She serves as a consultant of health care professionals as well as delivers direct service in psychotherapy. She has contributed to professional journals and is the author of *A Guide to Sexual Counseling: A Workbook Approach* (1977).